LEWIS
HAMILTON

Formula One Champion
2008 · 2014 · 2015

LEWIS HAMILTON

Formula One Champion
2008 · 2014 · 2015

BRUCE JONES

SevenOaks

First published in 2007 as
The Lewis Hamilton Story
Revised and updated in 2008

This edition published by Sevenoaks
an imprint of the Carlton Publishing Group
20 Mortimer Street
London W1T 3JW

10 9 8 7 6 5 4 3 2 1

A CIP catalogue record for this book is available
from the British Library.

ISBN: 978-1-78177-452-6

Design Manager: Luke Griffin
Designer: Katie Baxendale
Editorial Director: Martin Corteel
Picture Research: Paul Langan
Production: Lisa Cook

Printed in Dubai

>> The thrill of winning has never left Lewis, as
he shows in 2015 when his tally of 10 wins
landed him his third F1 title.

CONTENTS

INTRODUCTION

Britain has a unique relationship with its sporting stars. All too often, it builds them up then shoots them down if they should fail. Lewis Hamilton was their surefire ticket though, the black driver who was going to change the face of the sport. They jumped onto his bandwagon, as it was a question of when rather than if he became world champion. He was too good to fail. He was with McLaren, one of the top two teams. He was a fighter, a rookie driver who was putting noses out of joint. The media loved it, as he was magic, quicksilver. And, Lewis came within an ace of being crowned world champion at his first attempt.

That was in 2007, the adulation flowed. Then, as he gathered more wins in 2008, attitudes hardened. There were mistakes, races lost and suddenly the media was on his back and it became Lewis's championship to lose rather than to win. It was harsh, but it followed the newspapers' tried and tested formula of sparing the detail and making the headlines. You'd like to think that they wouldn't have turned on Lewis had he not scrabbled by Timo Glock's Toyota into the last corner on the final lap of the last race of 2008, but you can never be sure...

Fortunately, that nightmare scenario doesn't have to be contemplated, as he's done it, keeping the press onside, and the hundreds of thousands of young fans that he has brought into the sport in Britain alone can be allowed to revel in his glory, be inspired in all that he and his family have done in their ceaseless quest to achieve a dream. Celebration rather than recrimination is the order of the day.

It has been an amazing story. Turn back the clocks to 2007, and the headlines "rookie driver turns on the style", "rookie driver takes on the world champion," "rookie driver held back on the streets of Monaco" and "rookie driver turns winner" were emblazoned on the sports pages, front pages even, of newspapers around the world in Lewis's first season of Formula One. No first-year Formula One racer has ever made such an impact. With the wins flowing from June onwards, when he broke his duck in Montreal, Lewis established himself as the leader. This wasn't subterfuge, it was blatant leading from the front. He revitalised the sport, became an instant role model and gave the feeling that this was just the beginning of a trajectory that would make him to motor racing what world-beater Tiger Woods was to golf.

So rapid was his impact that his yellow crash helmet became the one that everyone would always look for as the pack of cars accelerated down to the first corner of a grand prix. Even on days when not everything went right, or the rival Ferrari team

>> Lewis is a hugely popular attraction wherever he goes and shows how intensely he cares for the fans by starring in a sure-to-be-treasured "selfie".

» Lewis the schoolboy racer was
something that could only happen
if Lewis met his side of a deal with
his father Anthony that his studying
must not be neglected.

"When the going gets tough, just keep on pushing. That's what I always do."

Lewis Hamilton

performed perfectly to assume control, Lewis would finish on the podium, making remarkably few mistakes even when under pressure and shattering records as he went. No rookie had ever been so successful, no career has ever looked so bright. It's true, too, that no other driver has ever subsumed the rest of the field into also-rans where the media are concerned. For 2007 at least, Lewis Hamilton was Formula One. You knew then that this was unsustainable, the other drivers becoming increasingly anti-Lewis as every question asked related to him, but there could be no doubting that this was the start of a very special Formula One career.

Prodigy is a description that can be overused, being apportioned to some who are good rather than great. Undeniably, Wolfgang Amadeus Mozart was a prodigy, composing music by the tender age of five. Against this, Lewis Carl Hamilton was something of a slow starter, although by any other frame of reference he was a trailblazer, an example to others, with eye-to-hand co-ordination that set him apart from his contemporaries. This and a will to win that was passed directly from his father Anthony. To whit, Lewis was beating adult radio-controlled car racers by the time he was seven.

That his parents wanted Lewis to be a child of world-beating potential could actually have been detected far earlier, as they were so impressed by multiple Olympic gold medal winner Carl Lewis that they simply transposed the American athlete's names when naming their son.

There can be no doubting that values are extremely important in the Hamilton household and the fact that they all stick to them is testament to the way that they have been applied. The family is exceptionally close, with the Anthony/Lewis, father/son relationship the most important dynamic in Lewis's life. It's the driving force behind every step that he has taken and every hurdle that he has cleared. Their climb to the top of the tree has certainly not been without struggle, as money was incredibly tight in the early days of his kart racing career, but they are all the stronger for this. Lewis and Anthony's journey has undoubtedly not been one of privilege, but one of focus and dedication, to say nothing of Lewis's ability being fine-tuned into a once-in-a-generation skill by incredible self-discipline and no little denial of the things that teenagers like to do. His passage to the top has been about looking, learning and applying and, ultimately, about maximising all the opportunities that came along once the McLaren Formula One team took its vital mentoring role.

Racing great Sir Stirling Moss – a man who can identify talent when he sees it – is of the opinion that Lewis is the best-prepared driver ever to reach Formula One and

"I was a racer, and he's one too. He's not only fast, just look at some of his overtaking manoeuvres."

Sir Stirling Moss

in this lies the secret to the way that Lewis hit the ground running when he made his debut in the Australian GP at Melbourne's Albert Park. It showed how Lewis did more than just take McLaren's money for the nine years since they signed him when he was just a 13-year-old kartist. He had honed his race skills, but also maximised everything in his approach to racing, learned as many lessons as he could about chassis set-up and data analysis, about the rules and regulations and also trained himself to be in peak fitness for this sapping job. Lewis is also a natural with the media, although his debut season was marked by McLaren holding him on a tight rein. This was frustrating for those wanting to write stories about the man who turned Formula One from all-white to multi-cultural, but it made sense as Lewis needed to be allowed to focus on the driving.

What has shone through, though, apart form his racer's instinct, is how normal a person Lewis is, how natural in all circumstances with a welcome lack of "front."

Indeed, Anthony has always kept Lewis's feet on the ground. Even when Lewis was world kart champion, the youngest ever as it happens, he made sure that he was out working in any down time to keep instilling the value of toil. This was in the valet bay of the local Mercedes dealership and Lewis's meticulous approach made his work stand out, which is just how Anthony liked it and it certainly left a mark on his work mates who recall him as a down-to-earth individual who was clearly going to go a long way in whatever he did.

One of the keys to Lewis's early years is that Anthony was exceptionally good at pushing Lewis forward. He put in considerable legwork to keep the show on the road and Lewis could not be other than impressed by his family's sacrifices. He was also fortunate that Anthony didn't fit the mould of the "karting dad", the sort who will scream at his child for failing to win and curse at anyone who prevents him from doing so. Best of all, Anthony has always asked for advice and taken heed of it.

Lewis attributes much of his success to the single-minded maxim of never giving up, saying: "When the going gets tough, just keep on pushing. That's what I always do." Some of his greatest races, when he has had to fight his way from the back to the front, such as the second GP2 race at Istanbul in 2006, give credence to that. To say nothing of how he fought to the very, and nearly bitter, end in Brazil to claim his crown.

It's not just all a matter of guts and application, and many of the sport's keenest insiders eulogise over Lewis's driving style, with his wide entry line, his smooth delivery and his ability to carry momentum through corners, even with the tail of the car out of

⌃ From the day he proved an instant hit in Formula One,
the media have followed Lewis's every move.

line. To those with a less trained eye, Lewis's results are enough to convince them of his merits.

When it comes to gauging how good a driver is, it makes the most sense to listen to the greats. Sir Stirling Moss is so excited by Lewis's talents that he is happy to compare his skills to his own teacher: five-time world champion Juan Manuel Fangio who was able to adapt to any machine in any conditions and still be fast: "In any era, there are four or five drivers with a realistic chance of winning, and Lewis became one of them straight away. I was a racer, and he's one too. He's not only fast, just look at some of his overtaking manoeuvres."

Sir Jackie Stewart is also a staunch supporter: "A real weakness within Formula One is that hardly any drivers believe that they need coaching," explains the three-time world champion. "Lewis is different. He has been coached all the way up the ladder and he's taken it all on board." Stewart, an individual of remarkable perception, went on to say that the majority of racing drivers are lethargic about everything outside the cockpit, but he was impressed that Lewis could all but recite the rule book back at him. In a sport in which success can be measured by thousandths of a second, every little counts, and the last driver to bother to harness all those extra little increments went on to collect seven Formula One titles. He was, of course, Michael Schumacher.

Throughout his career, the issue of Lewis's colour has been regarded as an extra, as a bonus rather than as the reason for his trajectory to the top, which is refreshing. Put plainly, the stopwatch doesn't lie: Lewis is an exceptional driver full stop. That he is black and successful has added new fans to the sport, but possibly not as many as those attracted simply by a new talent of world-beating class. Lewis is already a role-model of considerable appeal.

Speed and dedication aside, one of the most appealing attributes that Lewis displays is that he seems unchanged by success and the accompanying new-found fame, remaining open and honest whenever confronted by microphone or autograph-seeking fan. Long may he stay so. Indeed, Lewis has clear ideas of why he must always remain accessible. "When I was young," said Lewis, "some of the stars of the

"When I was young, some of the stars signed autographs without even looking at me. I'll never do that.

Lewis Hamilton

◀◀ Sporting a very Russian-styled Pirelli hat, Lewis celebrates the ninth win of his 2015 season, at Sochi, in a race in which his Mercedes team-mate Nico Rosberg failed to score.

day signed autographs without even looking at me. I'll never do that and always look children in the eye when I sign autographs for them. It's important." Too right, and so far he has practiced what he preaches, although his right arm really must have ached after the build-up to the British GP.

After landing that first F1 drivers' title in 2008, Lewis was hungry for more, but he was to learn that no team or driver is guaranteed to remain at the top of the pile, with McLaren being toppled in 2009 and Lewis winning just twice to tumble four places to end up ranked fifth overall. At the time, this was no doubt a dent in his expectations, but Brawn GP had found a technical advantage and Jenson Button had reaped the benefits. He wasn't to know it at the time, but he would go on to drive for the team in a different guise from 2013.

The key then was for McLaren to strike back in 2010 and Lewis's win tally went up by one, but this was good only for fourth overall in the closest finish to a season for decades as Sebastian Vettel came through in the final round to win the title with Red Bull Racing. Red Bull and Renault had the upper hand again in 2011, but by a far greater margin, and Lewis had to face up to being among the chasers, a situation that continued through 2012.

A change was clearly needed if Lewis wanted to be World Champion again, and so Lewis did what would have seemed unthinkable in 2007, and elected to leave McLaren, the team that had nurtured him through karts and taken him all the way to F1. Some felt that his choice of team for 2013 was surprising, as he switched to Mercedes, a team that had won nothing since the marque's return in 2010. But this was the team that had been Brawn GP in 2009, and, despite placing only fourth with just one victory, he outscored his team-mate Nico Rosberg in 2013, and better was to follow.

The improvement in 2014 as F1 changed to a radical new aero package and the use of smaller, turbocharged engines, was considerable. With the best equipment in his hands, Lewis truly delivered, winning 11 times. Becoming World Champion for a second time meant everything to Lewis and he was presented with another chance to go for gold in 2015. Rosberg proved a tougher opponent than before, but Lewis got the job done with three rounds still to run, wrapping up title number three at the United States GP with his 10th win of the season. This put Lewis level on three World Championships with Jack Brabham, Sir Jackie Stewart, Niki Lauda, Nelson Piquet and childhood hero Ayrton Senna, emphasising how he really is one of the greats of the sport.

Bruce Jones, March 2016

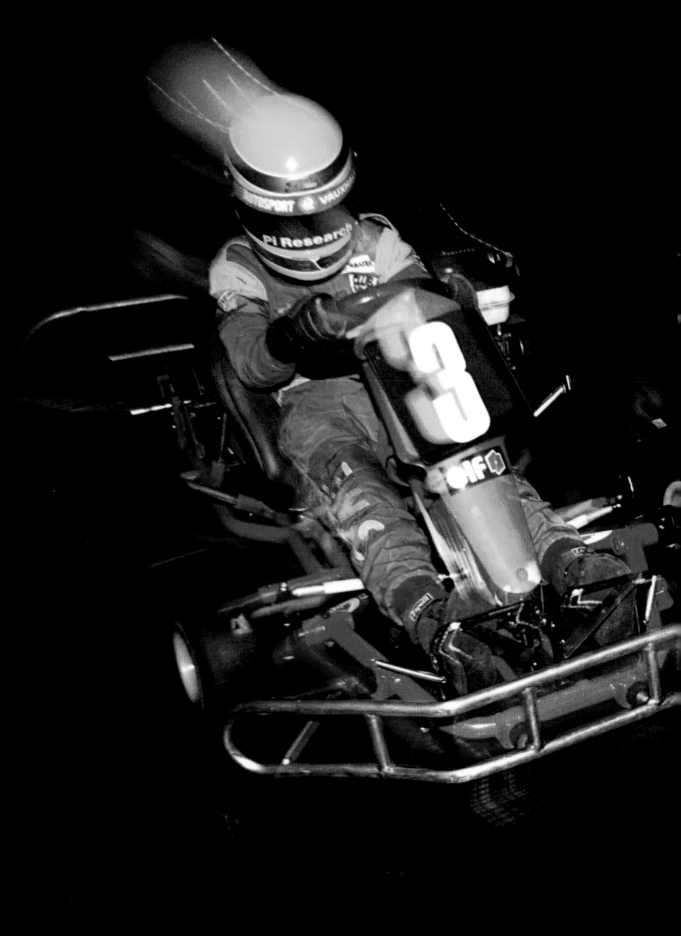

1. CHILD PRODIGY & BUDDING SUPERSTAR

CHILD PRODIGY & BUDDING SUPERSTAR

All babies are precious, but Lewis was especially precious when he was born in Tewin near Stevenage, Hertfordshire to Carmen and Anthony Hamilton on 7 January 1985, as they had spent years trying for a child. Lewis was two when they separated and he stayed with his mother on the Shephall estate, but life was tough.

Lewis's childhood passion was cars and Anthony bought him a radio-controlled car that he was soon racing. Such was his prowess, that Lewis was invited to appear on the BBC's *Blue Peter* children's television programme in 1992, on which he wiped the floor with his adult rivals. It might have appeared as a novelty to have a tiny seven-year-old performing with such aplomb, but the skill was there. It would be another year until Lewis found another outlet for his uncanny ability, and that was driving karts.

A pupil at Peartree Spring Infant School in Stevenage, Lewis was recalled by former headteacher Carol Hopkins first and foremost as a smiley and well-mannered boy. "He was a bright little button," she said, "but normal, very normal." Although popular with the teachers, Lewis suffered from bullying at school, perhaps for being different, for being black. To combat this, he took up karate and went on to gain an intermediate black belt.

This was indicative of the work ethos instilled in him by Anthony, whose family had come to Britain from Grenada in the 1950s, with his father Davidson looking to set the family on the road to a better life by working on the railways. That push to succeed was certainly passed down to Anthony and, in turn, to Lewis. When Carmen decided to quit Tewin for London when Lewis was 10, he moved in with his father, his stepmother Linda and stepbrother Nicolas. Lewis calls Nicolas, now 24, his biggest inspiration, and they are as close as brothers can be. Nicolas has cerebral palsy but remains cheerful and even competes in Touring Car Championship races in a specially modified car.

As fate would have it, one of the country's leading kart circuits, Rye House, was nearby, in Hoddesdon, and it was here that Anthony took eight-year-old Lewis in 1993, a visit that would shape the rest of his life. Cadet class racing is the bottom rung of the ladder, open to children to race once they turn eight. Powered by 60cc engines, there is a minimum weight for kart and driver combined and an upper age limit for participants of 12. Lewis was straight into the thick of the action, very much

>> You might see a sweet, gap-toothed little boy on a kart, but had you spoken to Lewis the cadet karter you would soon have realised his determination to win.

"The sort of raw talent to take driver to F1 is rare. There are only one or two a generation who are that good."
Circuit owner Bill Sisley

a cat among the pigeons. Novices are identified by racing with black plates on their kart for their first six races and it's rare to see them near the front of the field, Lewis was the exception from day one.

Martin Hines – former Superkart racing World Champion, boss of Britain's leading kart manufacturer Zip Kart and effective godfather of British kart racing for the past two decades – was a fan of Lewis's right from the very beginning. "I was there at Lewis's very first race at Rye House, as I was at the track running karts for my son Luke and Gary Paffett that day. We watched Lewis progress through the day and reckoned that he'd done really well as a novice. I went up to his father Anthony afterwards and asked him how many races Lewis had done. He amazed me when he said 'one', which made Lewis's speed even more impressive. So I told Anthony to come to my factory the next day as it was just down the road from them in Hoddesdon, and we got involved from there, giving technical and financial assistance as he drove our karts from then on."

Bill Sisley, managing director of the Buckmore Park kart circuit in Kent, was also sold on Lewis from the first day that he saw him race: "I have talent-spotted for 35 years and have always said that I can tell within two laps whether a young driver has what it takes, but the sort of raw talent that is enough to take them all the way to F1 is rare. There are only one or two in a generation who are that good. Lewis was one of them and his talent shouted out."

The cadet champion that year was Michael Spencer, who late became British Junior then Senior champion. He graduated to car racing and won the Zip Formula title in 2002 before racing against Lewis again in Formula Renault in 2003 when he showed flashes of form to end up eighth overall, but he dropped out of racing due to a lack of money.

Back for a second season of cadet karting in 1994, Niki Richardson raced to the title ahead of future touring car and British GT racer Luke Hines, but Lewis was increasingly competitive. He and Anthony developed together as a team, with son driving and father having to get to grips with the task of making sure that Lewis's kart hit the track in a competitive condition. This may have led to tensions, but both were focused enough to realise that they were working towards a common goal.

Still aged only 10, with up to two years of cadet kart racing open to him, Lewis raced in cadet karts again in 1995, and he proved that all the faith shown in his ability was well founded as he became the youngest ever British champion, adding the STP Cadet championship title for good measure.

▲ Success in the McLaren Mercedes Champions of the Future series is what propelled Lewis towards the top of karting, starting with his cadet title in 1996.

Also in 1995 another major landmark in his life came when Carmen decided to move to London and Lewis chose, since karting was everything to him and Anthony was the one who made it happen, to stay on in Stevenage in a one-bedroomed flat... Carmen has since admitted that she would not have been able to afford to keep Lewis's adored karting career on track. Anthony was the mover and shaker in that department, so Lewis stayed with him.

Knowing that he was going to have to do something different to earn more money to keep Lewis's burgeoning karting career on track, Anthony chose this moment to take redundancy from his job at British Rail and so started his famous stint of holding down three jobs simultaneously just to pay the bills. This was a difficult period, with time at a premium as he drove Lewis all over the country to the races, but the wheels stayed on the wagon, just.

In 1996, McLaren fittingly took an interest in up-and-coming stars by sponsoring the McLaren Mercedes Champions of the Future series that had been instigated by Martin Hines. It stood out from other karting championships not just because it had the involvement of a top Formula One team, but because it was televised. This was where all aspiring kart stars wanted to do their winning, a never-before-seen shop-window for their talents and hopefully an arena in which they could attract sponsorship to help them advance up the motor racing ladder.

Lewis became cadet champion again, adding the Sky TV Kart Masters and Five Nations titles.

The television coverage also gave Lewis a chance to hone another facet of his portfolio: appearing in front of TV cameras. As a frequent race winner, there were plenty of interviews to do and thus plenty of opportunities to prove what a well-adjusted and natural young man he was, at the age of 11...

Television presenter and radio DJ David "Kid" Jensen fronted the show and suggested that Lewis's name would one day be on the side of a Formula One car as he stood out not just for his speed but for his natural way that was always appealing, never arrogant.

"My dad can be really hard on me. But, at the end of the day, we're a team and we'll make it."

Lewis Hamilton

⌃ Little Lewis at the *Autosport* Awards with Williams Formula One driver Jacques Villeneuve in December 1996, the night that he met Ron Dennis.

This was also the year that Lewis moved up to secondary school, to the John Henry Newman Catholic School in Stevenage, where he again went quietly about his business, but was able to compare his sporting progress with that of another incredibly focused and talented class-mate, Ashley Young, who was soon being spotted by footballing scouts and is now starring for Aston Villa. Lewis also played midfield, but he realised that compared to Young his best hopes of hitting the top lay in four-wheeled sport rather than on the football field.

One of the key moments in Lewis's burgeoning career came that December, when Lewis made a major impression on a very important person when he attended the end-of-year *Autosport* Awards dinner at the Grosvenor House Hotel on London's Park Lane to collect a trophy. This VIP was McLaren principal Ron Dennis. On being asked later for his autograph and a drive with McLaren in the future, Dennis looked down, smiled and wrote into Lewis's autograph book "call me again in nine years." A few years later, though, it was Dennis who picked up the telephone, but more of that later...

Martin Hines takes up the story. "Lewis was on our table at the *Autosport* Awards as one of the McLaren Mercedes Champions of the Future title winners," reports the Zip Kart boss. "I took him, Gary (Paffett) – who had won the Senior McLaren Mercedes Champions of the Future title – and my son Luke up to speak to Ron [Dennis] after the presentations and suggested that he got them all under contract. Ten years later, both Lewis and Gary are McLaren drivers." Gary was a test driver for McLaren until 2014.

For 1997, as he was about to exceed the age limit for cadets, Lewis moved up to the Junior Yamaha class for racers aged between 12 and 16. Lewis took to these more powerful karts like a duck to water, racing to the McLaren Mercedes Champions of the Future and British Super One championship titles. Backed by Pi Research – a company owned by Tony Purnell who would go on to run Jaguar Racing in years to come – Lewis was soon in among the winners.

When Lewis appeared on *Blue Peter* again he said: "Racing against people older than me is quite a challenge as they know the tracks better than me and they've

With the backing of McLaren Mercedes, Lewis cut a swathe through the ranks of senior karting, all the way to becoming the youngest ever world number one.

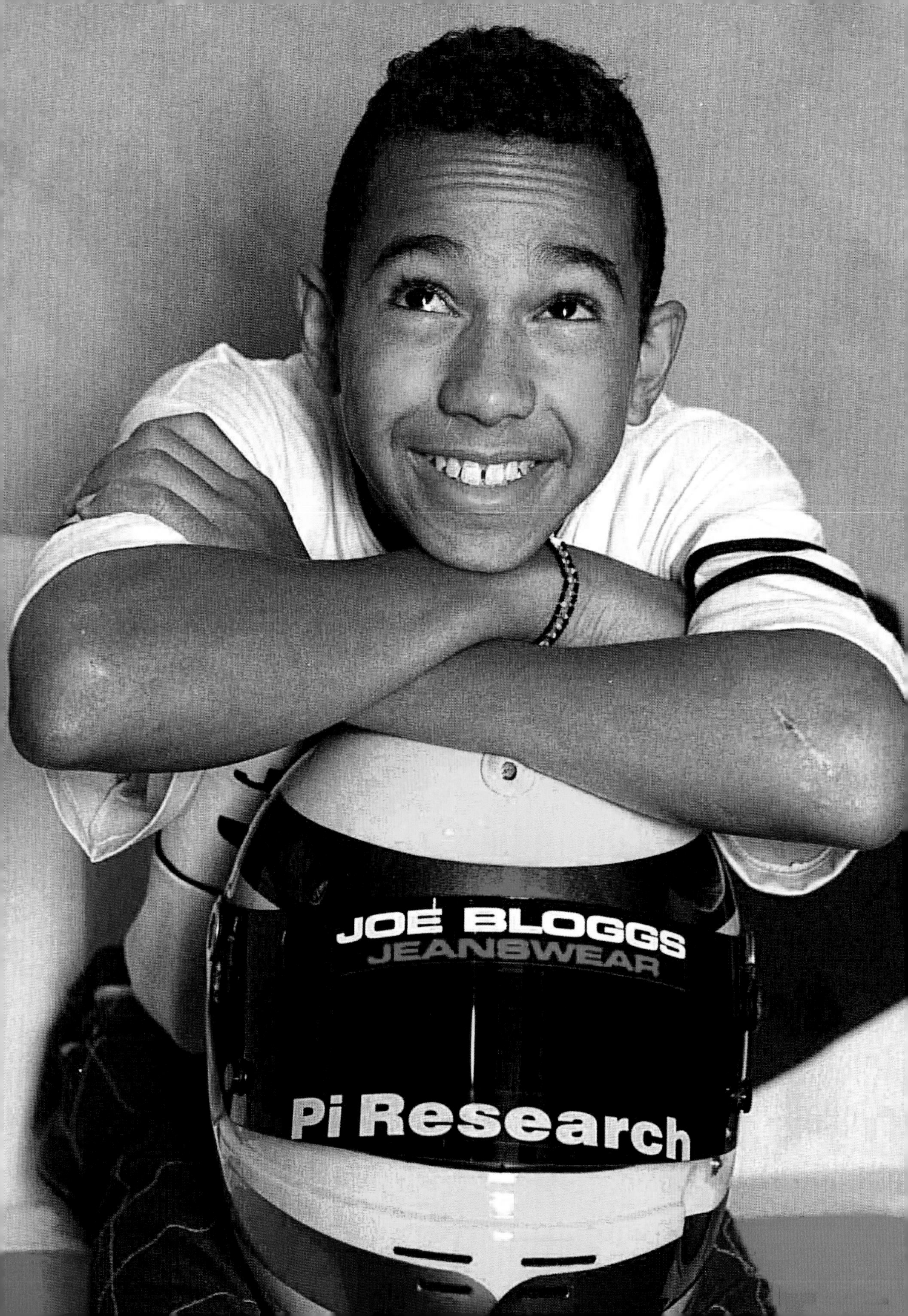
JOE BLOGGS
JEANSWEAR
Pi Research

Lewis, still a cadet kart racer, poses with Niki Cleland, son of British Touring Car Champion John Cleland.

The Pi Research logo on Lewis's visor identifies this as 1997, when Lewis stepped up from cadets to the more powerful Junior Yamaha class.

been racing longer, but I'm beating them." Others might have laughed at this moment, but Lewis was deadly serious. Kart racing was fun, but it wasn't a game to him. There wasn't room on the track for sentiments, as Lewis went on to explain, saying: "I've got a lot of friends in karting, but when we're out on the track they're not my friends as I'm out to get them."

When quizzed about what it was like being run by his father, Lewis explained that this too meant running outside a child's normal comfort zone from time to time. "My Dad can be really hard on me," said Lewis. "When things aren't going to plan, he's even harder. But, at the end of the day, we're a team and we'll make it."

Anthony had clear ideas of why Lewis might just make it: "He's very determined and does not like losing. That's why he wins."

Win he did and Lewis kept on moving up, but ascending the rungs of the karting ladder means taking on more power, and when Lewis stepped up to JICA (Junior Intercontinental A) in 1998, he was racing a kart powered by a 100cc piston-ported engine in a class for 13 to 16-year-olds. Karting was now getting really serious.

The most important event related to 1998 was that Lewis landed support from the McLaren Mercedes Formula One team. Yes, the telephone call that McLaren boss Ron Dennis made came, offering to help with Lewis's career, with the end goal being Formula One. Of course reaching Formula One was Lewis's ambition too, but it seemed a long, long way off. Yet, here was the boss of the pre-eminent team offering to help get him there. It was almost unbelievable. Thus Lewis became the youngest ever driver contracted to a Formula One team and he would never race with equipment other than the best from then on.

The phone call came after Lewis and Andrew Delahunty – a winner of one of the previous year's McLaren Mercedes Champions of the Future titles – were taken to the Belgian Grand Prix as part of their prize. It was at Spa-Francorchamps at the end of August 1997, seemingly, that Dennis decided that he really liked what he saw in Lewis. The telephone call he made early in 1998 meant that Anthony, who was

McLaren Formula One team boss Ron Dennis poses with Lewis when he was a guest of the team at the 1997 Belgian Grand Prix at Spa-Francorchamps.

already holding down three jobs to finance Lewis's karting, might be able to back off a little. Indeed, Anthony was subsequently able to establish his own IT consultancy, from which he has since made a fortune. It shows that champions' genes are deep in the Hamilton DNA.

After the deal was done with McLaren Mercedes, Lewis told a television news reporter where he was heading: "My ambition is to get to Formula One. I enjoy the speed, and would like to be with all the big guys and to be making lots of money." The sentiments were clear, concise and focused, particularly as they were the words of a 13-year-old. But no one could ever have guessed just how much Lewis would earn in F1.

Armed with vital financing for his 1998 campaign, Anthony felt he should spend it wisely, to impress McLaren that he wasn't being profligate with their money. So he and Lewis followed the course taken by numerous champions before him, including David Coulthard, Anthony Davidson and Paffett, by signing to be a full member of Zip Kart's Young Guns team under the guidance of Martin Hines.

"You could say that Ron Dennis made Lewis, or I did by helping him in karts," said Hines, "but actually the only reason that Lewis is where he is today, winning grands prix for McLaren, is the little man behind the wheel: Lewis himself."

"People ask me constantly what Lewis is like," he continued, "and I tell them that he's the same today as he was as a 10-year-old. They also ask whether he's cut out to take the pressure, but I can guarantee that a driver who has lined up as a 10-year-old in front of a television audience of millions having to win a race to secure a championship can cope with pressure. I don't think it will ever get to Lewis."

Even though Lewis was once again stepping up a category, he proved the maxim that "class will out", ending the 1998 season as runner-up in the McLaren Mercedes Champions of the Future series behind Frazer Sheader, emphasising just how competitive he could be even against drivers who were several years older than him at a stage of life where a few years can seem like an eternity as puberty hits and leaves boys racing against young adults.

Lewis also started racing abroad in 1998, as Anthony wanted Lewis to take on the best of his contemporaries so that he could continue not only to learn his craft but

> **"My ambition is to get to Formula One. I enjoy the speed and would like to be with the big guys."**
>
> **Lewis Hamilton**

❯❯ Prince Charles looks suitably entertained by something that the 14-year-old Lewis has said to him when the Prince of Wales visited McLaren's headquarters in Woking.

"Whenever Lewis went on the track, he would win. He was always fastest."

Kieran Crawley, kart mechanic

also the circuits on which he'd need to shine if he was to work his way successfully through the senior kart categories in the years ahead before graduating to car racing. To this end, Anthony signed mechanic Kieran Crawley to look after him as he went off to race for TopKart, for whom Zip Kart is the British distributor. With Lewis being only 13 years old, Kieran also had to act as his chaperone when Anthony wasn't around, making sure that Lewis didn't get into any trouble. Not that Lewis would have done, as success at karting was everything and he appreciated just how much his father was putting into his career.

Crawley was impressed from the start of their relationship, telling James Corrigan of *The Independent*: "The first day we went to the track, we were talking and I had to check myself and remember that Lewis was just a kid and I was 25. He could hold a conversation as good as any of my friends."

Lewis's European forays culminated in finishing fourth in the Italian Open series, with some valuable experience gained.

The 1999 season proved yet another good one as Lewis stepped up to ICA – the Intercontinental A class for faster-revving reed-valve engined karts – to race a CRG kart for TeamMBM.com, run by 1982 Formula One champion Keke Rosberg. "That was quite a coincidence," said Hines, "as I'd raced against Keke in karts before he started racing cars and now here was Lewis, who I'd helped out, racing with Keke's son Nico. Also, after I ran Gary [Paffett] in the British Formula Three Championship the following year, Keke's team fielded him in the German series."

Lewis won the Italian ICA championship with team-mate Nico being runner-up. Fifteen years later, Lewis and Nico were not only Mercedes Formula One team-mates but also first and second, respecivtely, in the Drivers' World Championship!

Crawley knew their respective merits: "Whenever Lewis went on the track he would win. He was always fastest. Against Nico, it was close, but Nico would always come second. It was a great feeling turning up knowing that we were going to win."

In addition to that Italian ICA title, Lewis was also European JICA series runner-up, with Rosberg ranked fourth overall.

The 2000 season was Lewis's crowning glory in karts as he advanced to the yet more powerful Formula A category and became the youngest ever World number one, aged just 15½. Already European Formula A champion, after winning each of the four rounds ahead of Rosberg and future Formula One rival Robert Kubica, and winner of the second round of the Italian Open series, Lewis was crowned World Cup champion at Motegi in Japan.

Anthony is the proudest of fathers and every additional trophy added to Lewis's collection made clear to him that all of his sacrifices were worthwhile.

Lewis finished the season with the Elf Masters, an invitation race against the world's best Formula Three car racers at the Bercy indoor stadium outside Paris. He beat all-comers, leaving Crawley with one last memory of their time together: "He was only 15, but he whupped all these professionals, all these adults. They were amazed at what he'd just done, yet all Lewis wanted to do was look at the girls. The talent was obvious, the speed was obvious and everyone knew where he'd end up. To be honest, as soon as McLaren got involved, all he had to do was work hard. It was a case of when, not if."

Lewis's school friends were increasingly aware of his success in karting, aware that he might actually be able to make a career out of his racing, but what probably impressed them the most was in his GCSE year when he arrived in a Mercedes with his name emblazoned on its flanks, courtesy of that patronage deal with McLaren. That really meant something to those who cared not a jot for motor racing.

As reigning World Champion, Lewis raced on in Formula A in 2001, but his focus was already on stepping up to car racing as soon as he could, with plans to kick off in cars that November. First, though, he stuck to his side of a bargain with his father of "no study, no karting" and moved that September to the Cambridge College of Arts and Science to study for his A-Levels. Here, Lewis met his girlfriend, Jodia Ma.

At the end of that October, Lewis contested the final round of the World Championship on Michael Schumacher's home track at Kerpen in Germany. As well as his usual rivals Rosberg and Vitantonio Liuzzi, the great Schumacher – already a five-time Formula One World Champion back then – took part in the event. He finished second and Lewis was a disappointed seventh after a handful of problems, but Michael had seen enough to be deeply impressed, saying: "He's a quality driver, very strong and only 16. If he keeps this up I'm sure he will reach F1. It's something special to see a kid of his age out on the circuit. He's clearly got the right racing mentality." It takes a champion to know one.

So, Lewis's kart career was over. It had been garlanded from start to finish, his name cut onto hundreds of trophies. Rivals may have been jealous because of McLaren Mercedes's backing, but Lewis had usually made the best use of it. Now, he had to make similar headway through single-seaters in pursuit of his F1 dreams.

The Hamilton/Rosberg partnership didn't start in F1 in 2013, but in karts in 1999. Here, Lewis carries his trophies at Bercy in 2000.

This wonderful onboard camera shot shows Lewis at the wheel in the indoor Elf Masters event at Bercy in 2000 when he put down his marker.

In November 2001, Lewis, still only 16½, moved to the next stage of his passage towards his Formula One, entering the car racing scene to contest the two-meeting, four-race British Formula Renault Winter Series. Manor Motorsport signed Lewis, with team owner John Booth keen to give him a few outings ahead of a full season in 2002.

It didn't start well; Lewis put the car into the barriers after three laps of his first test session at Mallory Park and then crashed out of his first race.

"When we tested Lewis in late 2001, he was only 16, just a kid," said Booth. "We didn't know what to expect, but he was very mature and quiet. He had one little bump in that first test, but he was full of confidence. And we liked him, as Lewis was the kind of guy even then that people take to."

Fortunately, his raw speed was there for all to see at Rockingham when Lewis took fourth place in the second of the opening pair of races and then this was backed up by a fifth place finish at Donington Park to leave Lewis ranked fifth overall. Champion Rob Bell – who was six years older – won all four races. It must be remembered though that Lewis was just dipping his toe in the water of the car racing pond and Manor Motorsport team manager Tony Shaw was impressed by his attacking style and his sheer confidence. All Lewis's car craft needed was a little finesse.

"Between those winter series and the start of the 2002 season, he only came up to see us once [at our Yorkshire base] for a seat-fitting," continued Booth, "But don't forget that back then he was too young to drive on the road and had to rely on his father to take him everywhere."

Lewis started well, with a third place in the opening round at Brands Hatch before qualifying only ninth at Oulton Park next time out and then falling to 15th place by flagfall after one of the mistakes that characterised his early races. This wasn't fitting in with Lewis's career trajectory, but then progress was made with second place at Thruxton behind Mark McLoughlin before he tripped up at Silverstone and was

Formula Renault was Lewis's first step in car racing. He was a winner in his ninth start when he got everything right for Manor Motorsport at Thruxton in 2002.

« **"" We didn't know what to expect of Lewis, but he was very mature and quiet, and full of confidence. ""**

John Booth

placed only ninth, albeit with the race's fastest lap to his name. This was a theme that would continue through Lewis's ascent to the top, with a period of adjustment required before Lewis started hitting the high notes.

Success in motorsport can be achieved by finding the tiniest of advantages but then achieving that extra increment again and again, and so it proved as the mistakes stopped at the fifth round, at Thruxton, when Lewis boosted his confidence with victory from pole position ahead of the Fortec Motorsport duo Jamie Green and Danny Watts at this high-speed circuit. Two more wins would follow, at Brands Hatch and Donington Park, but Watts was almost never off the podium and ended the season as champion, while the more consistent Green edged Lewis into third place.

"He could have sneaked past Green at the last round to be runner-up," said Booth. "The speed was always there, but perhaps Lewis's biggest problem in 2002 was qualifying when he always wanted to find 2s when we fitted new tyres, rather than just 0.2s. That summed up his desire to be fastest every time he went out in the car. You could explain it to him, but as soon as the helmet went on he was on his own and would go out to blow everyone away."

It's said in motor racing that your best yardstick is your team-mate. This suggests Lewis's first full season of car racing was a clear success as he outperformed the other three Manor Motorsport drivers, with American Patrick Long eighth, Irish racer Matt Griffin 11th and Venezuelan hopeful Ernesto Viso 20th. Long only became a race winner when he transferred to Fortec Motorsport.

Manor Motorsport also entered Lewis in the Formula Renault Euro Cup and he scored a brace of second-place finishes and a victory at Donington Park to rank fifth overall despite entering just four of the championship's nine rounds.

With his 18th birthday approaching in 2003, Lewis and Manor Motorsport were back for more Formula Renault, his silver over black car bearing TAG Heuer sponsorship. Success was needed to satisfy the ambitions of Lewis, Anthony and mentors McLaren Mercedes. Anything less than the outright title would be seen as failure.

McLaren didn't apply overt pressure, though, according to Booth: "They sent two engineers up to watch over one of our rounds, but our main contact was that [Chief Executive Officer] Martin Whitmarsh would phone for a chat after every fifth round or so. It was very relaxed from McLaren actually, and the pressure came from within, from Lewis's desire to be the best."

Despite the experience Lewis gained in 2002, it took until the fifth round for Lewis to start winning, when he became the fifth different winner in this most closely-fought

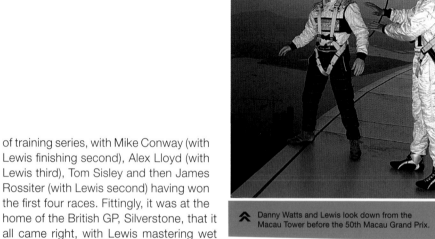

Danny Watts and Lewis look down from the Macau Tower before the 50th Macau Grand Prix.

of training series, with Mike Conway (with Lewis finishing second), Alex Lloyd (with Lewis third), Tom Sisley and then James Rossiter (with Lewis second) having won the first four races. Fittingly, it was at the home of the British GP, Silverstone, that it all came right, with Lewis mastering wet conditions on his slick tyres to beat Sisley to the chequered flag by half a second.

Once that victory was in the bag, Lewis won another nine times to finish the season as British champion. None of his early-season rivals could counter the charge, while team-mates Sergio Jimenez and Matthew Wilson ranked only 11th and 18th. Former kart rival Michael Spencer raced against Lewis again through 2003 and surmised that there was one particular key to Lewis's success: "He was always so fast over the first three laps of a race. You might be able to catch up again as the race went on, but he'd already done the damage by being so fast on cold tyres."

As in the autumn of 2001 when Lewis tried a few Formula Renault races at the tail-end of the season with an eye to progressing the following year, Lewis and Manor Motorsport went to Brands Hatch for the final round of the British Formula Three Championship, a series that had produced many future world champions and grand prix winners. He didn't win; in fact, he ended in hospital with concussion, but Lewis had been fastest of all in wet pre-event testing and again in qualifying until he crashed and the subsequent red flag ruled out a time that would have put him an astounding fourth on the grid, so his natural speed had impressed everybody who witnessed it.

Lewis was ready for the next step and took pole for an international Formula Three race in Korea, proving he could take on the best as the season came to a close.

The logical, time-honoured step would have been to enter the British Formula Three Championship in 2004, now that he knew the circuits well. It would have been good to add his name to the list of champions, which included Ayrton Senna, Mika Hakkinen and Rubens Barrichello, but he, McLaren and Manor Motorsport reckoned a year spent in Europe would be more career-enhancing and so he entered the European Formula Three series. The idea was that Lewis would get acquainted with the circuits that he would need to know when he graduated to the sport's top categories. Making matters slightly tricky were the facts that Manor Motorsport had never run a European campaign before and Dutch driver Charles Zwolsman was not

"Lewis was always so fast over the first three laps of a race."

Formula Renault rival Michael Spencer

a competitive enough team-mate to help develop the car. In a category as technical as Formula Three, where a minimal change in chassis set-up can make a massive difference to lap times, and a class where engine horsepower is limited, drivers simply aren't able to drive around a chassis deficiency, this was something of a handicap.

Lewis had a sizeable shunt at Hockenheim in pre-season testing. and made a slow start to the season, with a best finish of fourth place in the first of the two races at Pau in round four. But skill will out, and Lewis claimed victory in the fifth double-header round, held on the Norisring street circuit in Nuremburg. He started the first race from pole ahead of Nicolas Lapierre and Alexandre Premat, before heading home a third French driver, Loic Duval, by a couple of seconds. In the second race, Premat won from Jamie Green, with Lewis third.

Backed up with three third-place finishes and a second behind French ace Lapierre at the final race meeting at Hockenheim, Lewis ended his European Formula Three campaign fifth overall, ranked behind ASM's Green and Premat, Lapierre plus Nico Rosberg. Team-mate Zwolsman was way off Lewis's pace, ending up 16th overall.

"His pre-season shunt might have put Lewis on the back foot a bit," opined Booth, "but he came good in the second half of the year. He didn't become faster, but simply refined that speed and it all came together."

Armed with this experience, Lewis headed east at season's end to compete in the Formula Three invitation race at Macau, just down the Chinese coast from Hong Kong. This is, without doubt, the toughest street circuit in the world, and its victory roll contains Senna, Michael Schumacher and David Coulthard. Lewis won the qualifying race ahead of Rosberg, Premat, the pole-starting Robert Kubica (Lewis's team-mate for the meeting) and Green, but it all went wrong early in the main race.

Rosberg had outdragged Lewis away from the start and led onto the second lap. He was too busy looking in his mirrors to see if Lewis was about to attack, braked too late into a constricting right-hand bend, Lisboa, and slammed into the tyrewall. As if in sympathy, Lewis also locked up and Premat dived past to take a lead that he wouldn't lose, even after clouting a barrier and bending his rear suspension. Rosberg was out on the spot, while Lewis dived up the escape road, turned around and rejoined way down the order. He dragged himself back into the top ten, but a late-race clash with Kazuki Nakajima cost him, and he came home a chastened 14th.

Straight after this, though, Lewis achieved what would be the life's ambition for most young racers: he had a run in a McLaren Formula One car at Silverstone. He was joined there by rivals Green and Alex Lloyd, both winners of the annual McLaren

↗ Father Anthony has been at Lewis's side from day one in karting in 1993, but he does more than simply advise, working his son's corner to devastating effect.

↗↗ Lewis learned new circuits in 2004 by contesting the Formula 3 Euroseries. Here, he congratulates runner-up Loic Duval after they came first and second in the first race at the Norisring.

Autosport BRDC Award, a scholarship for junior British drivers, but this was something for which Lewis was ineligible, having raced at Formula Three. Lewis enjoyed his experience at Silverstone, but for him, it was a just another step towards his ultimate goal, that of laying down his name as the greatest driver ever.

McLaren Chief Executive Officer Martin Whitmarsh was impressed: "We are all particularly delighted for Lewis that he has had this one-off opportunity. It has been a competitive season and this is a fitting reward for all the hard work that he has put in to maintain his steep learning curve." You sort of felt that this wouldn't be the last time that Lewis ever got to venture onto a circuit in a Formula One car...

After Silverstone, Lewis went to Bahrain for Formula Three's season-closing Superprix. It appeared as if it was one trip too many as Lewis was caught out by the wet conditions. Yes, it rained in the desert, and his off-track excursion damaged the floor of the car, leaving Lewis 21st of the 31 starters. Fortunately, there was a qualifying race to decide the starting order for the Superprix and Lewis halved his job by climbing to 11th in this as European champion Green controlled proceedings.

What followed in the Superprix was truly remarkable as Lewis rattled past his rivals as though they weren't there. Don't forget, too, that Formula Three is famously a category in which little overtaking is done because the margin between the drivers is so close. Lewis was fourth by the time the field poured out of the first corner, with Green and Rosberg fighting over the lead and Fabio Carbone the next driver in his sights. Lewis's task was made easier when the Safety Car was deployed and he made a blinding restart to climb straight to second, behind only Green. However, Lewis's tyres had paid the price for his furious attacks and he was unable to resist an attack from Rosberg, until the Safety Car was called out again, bunching the field once more. This time, Lewis was gifted the lead on the restart when Green hesitated slightly, surprised by the Safety Car's sudden withdrawal, and Rosberg made a move at the hairpin. The leading two ran wide, leaving all the gap that Lewis needed to complete his rise from 21st to first and give himself the perfect momentum into the close-season. This race alone proved that Lewis was not only quicker than his rivals, but also he was a better racer and it ended his season on the highest of high notes.

❝❝To win at Pau, Spa and Monaco in a couple of weeks is something special.❞❞

**Mercedes Motorsport boss
Nortbert Haug**

That was the end of Lewis's time as a driver with Manor Motorsport, but he did keep in contact with John Booth's team. He wanted to move straight up to Formula One feeder category GP2 for 2005, but long-time backers McLaren Mercedes felt he would benefit more from staying on and winning the European Formula Three crown. Lewis duly complied, and started the year as the firm favourite, especially as he had joined ASM, the team that had helped Green to win the 2004 crown, with team-mate Premat as runner-up.

Run by Frederic Vasseur, ASM was the premier outfit. With a competitive team-mate in Adrian Sutil to spur him on further, Lewis hit the ground running by winning the opening race at Hockenheim and then storming to the title with 15 wins in 20 starts, usefully with victories on four circuits (Hockenheim, Spa-Francorchamps, Monaco and the Nurburgring) that host Formula One grands prix. With only a few more than half of Lewis's points tally of 172, Sutil, on 94, finished the year as runner-up ahead of Lucas di Grassi (68), Franck Perera (67) and Sebastian Vettel (63). To dominate the championship to the extent that Lewis had was quite remarkable and this confirmed the 20-year-old as one of the hottest talents to emerge from Formula Three since Jan Magnussen blitzed the British series in 1994. The Dane did reach Formula One, but his career never fulfilled the early potential.

Lewis's 2005 European Formula Three season highlights included winning around the famous Pau street circuit in south-west France, taking wins at Spa and Monaco then beating all-comers at the Masters event at Zandvoort on the Dutch coast where an even more youthful Vettel proved to be the best of the rest.

Mercedes Motorsport boss Norbert Haug was deeply impressed: "To win at Pau, Spa and Monaco in a couple of weeks, and to win on such classic circuits in such a short space of time is something special."

Asked whether there had been pressure from McLaren to continue to show a return on their investment, Lewis told *Autosport* magazine that there was pressure, but it was more supportive than overt. He noted that as everything that McLaren wanted was also what he wanted, there was just as much pressure from within.

So, with European Formula Three title added to his curriculum vitae, Lewis now reached the the final step before Formula One, GP2 and, for 2006, he joined ART Grand Prix, a team co-owned by Vasseur and Ferrari chief Jean Todt's son Nicolas. Lewis took over the seat vacated by friend and 2005 champion, Nico Rosberg.

Nicolas Todt was excited by the prospect, saying: "Lewis has proved in all of the junior formulae that he has a natural talent for driving and has displayed great

It's not only British tracks that get hit by rain... Lewis splashes his way to victory at Spa in 2005 ahead of ASM team-mate Adrian Sutil.

professionalism. We are thrilled to be able to count on his pure speed and maturity." He was clearly right to feel such excitement, but quite how he felt knowing that Lewis would probably drive for McLaren one day against his father's Ferrari team isn't known, although he had no choice but to pick Lewis if he wanted to have the best shot at the GP2 title.

With its identical cars, GP2 is designed to be competitive and to give the best driver, rather than the wealthiest team or competitor, the opportunity to win. Even by GP2's standards, though, the category was to enjoy an unusually competitive season in 2006, studded as it was with talents such as Lewis's team-mate Premat who had ranked fourth overall in GP2 in 2005 behind Rosberg, Heikki Kovalainen and Scott Speed, plus Nelson Piquet Jr as well as Formula One refugees Timo Glock, Giorgio Pantano and Gianmaria Bruni and other hopefuls Michael Ammermuller, Adam Carroll and Nicolas Lapierre from Germany, Britain and France, respectively. As all but one of GP2's 10 rounds were the lead support race for Formula One grands prix, success was doubly worth achieving being witnessed by Formula One team chiefs, not that Lewis's progress hadn't gone unnoticed to this point in his garlanded career.

Piquet Jr set the ball rolling in April by winning the opening GP2 round at Valencia for his family team ahead of Lewis, then Ammermuller won the second race of the Spanish double-header for Arden International. The next meeting, at Imola, was a disaster for Lewis, as he was disqualified from the first race for passing the Safety Car, and finishing only 10th in the second race, with the wins going to Bruni for Trident Racing and Lewis's 2002 Formula Renault team-mate Ernesto Viso for iSport International. However, a brace of wins at the Nurburgring put Lewis onto the attack and after losing out to team-mate Premat and Viso at Barcelona, Lewis demonstrated his affinity for Monaco by winning there. The momentum was with him and his white car with its red stripe up its nose was very much the one to beat.

As a driver who had not raced in Britain since 2003, and thus hadn't fully been picked up by the radars of occasional British race-goers, Lewis then displayed a showman's touch to win both races in front of their largest gathering for the GP2 races supporting the British GP at Silverstone. He won the first of these by passing Racing Engineering's pole-sitter Carroll into the first corner. As per the GP2 regulations, the

"Our objective was to win both titles, and now it is done and done well."

GP2 team boss Frederic Vasseur

top eight finishers start race two in reverse order, so Lewis had some passing to do as he attempted to win from eighth on the grid.

Those who were there will long remember his three-abreast overtaking manoeuvre at Becketts when he entered the esses behind DPR Direxiv's Clivio Piccione and Piquet Jr and yet emerged at the other end of the high-speed sequence of bends in front. No other driver would even have considered such a move. Then again, as people saw in Formula One in 2007, he is the king of overtaking, the master passer. Lewis duly went on to hunt down pole-starter and race leader Felix Porteiro. Records show his victory was by 10s from compatriot Carroll, but only because Porteiro was disqualified from second place thanks to an irregularity with his car's steering rack. However, it was the nature of Lewis's victory rather than the final margin that lingers longest in the memories of those who saw it.

It seemed impossible that Lewis could top this, but top it he did, with a truly astonishing comeback drive in the penultimate round in Istanbul, Turkey, fighting back from 16th place after a spin to an eventual second behind Austrian driver Andreas Zuber in the Sunday race to help ART to land its second straight teams' title, with Premat ending up third overall in the championship standings behind Piquet Jr.

By finishing third in the first of the two races at the Monza finale, behind Fisichella Motorsport International's Pantano and Piquet Jr, Lewis clinched the title. For good measure, he raced to second in the closing race, pushing Pantano all the way to the chequered flag, to leave his eventual margin over Piquet Jr at 12 points.

ART boss Vasseur was more than satisfied: "Our objective at the start of the year was to win both titles and now it is done and done well." Indeed it was.

Understandably, Lewis was also delighted at clearing his final hurdle before the big time: "It has been an amazing season, a sensational rollercoaster. There have been so many highlights and now the next target is to win the Formula One World Championship." And he wasn't kidding.

The strangest thing about Lewis reaching the end of his ascent towards Formula One was that anyone still had any doubts over his abilities. Yet, despite his success in almost every class since his first steps in cadet karting, there are still some in the sport who largely ignore all that goes before Formula One, and these were the ones who were most shocked by what happened when he did arrive...

2. THE FORMULA ONE SEASON 2007

THE FORMULA ONE
SEASON 2007

As Lewis looked ahead to 2007, with one McLaren seat thrown open by Juan Pablo Montoya's departure to race NASCAR stock cars in the USA, the crux was for whom he would race. Although he was contracted to McLaren apparently through until 2011, that didn't guarantee Lewis a race seat. Certainly, it was a relationship that had done him nothing but favours for a decade, but now was the time of reckoning and any hesitation might hold him back. However, perhaps aware that he might walk if he was offered only a test driver's role as this would interrupt his career momentum and perhaps leave him up a cul-de-sac, McLaren broke with a long-standing habit at the end of November and offered this rookie a race seat for 2007 alongside double world champion Fernando Alonso who was moving across from Renault. Some questioned whether it was right to put a rookie in alongside a double world champion. Lewis had no fears about the outcome and nor did Ron Dennis.

"We reviewed the whole grid," Dennis told the press, "and when we looked at the drivers other than the top three [Alonso, the retiring Michael Schumacher and Ferrari-bound Raikkonen], we felt that they had pretty much reached a plateau in their careers and there was no one who really shone. In looking at Lewis both in and out of the car, he's a very polished ambassador for McLaren Mercedes and worthy of having the opportunity of showing what he can do."

Lewis, for his part, wasn't fazed by the thought of being paired with Alonso, telling *Autosport* magazine: "I feel extremely positive about it. I think the stronger the team-mate, the better. It makes you have to work even harder and I'm willing to work as hard as is needed to get to the top of my game and to beat him. If I'm given the same car, anything is possible."

With the paperwork inked, Lewis kicked off at Barcelona by putting in some serious miles for McLaren to set the ball rolling for 2007, with every lap needing to count as he gathered vital mileage.

There was more testing, including one stopped short when he crashed at Valencia, more horsepower to play with, more PR duties and certainly more media exposure than ever before. So, by the time Lewis reached Melbourne for the season-opening Australian GP, he simply wanted to get out there to do what he does best: driving. He drove well, too, ending up third fastest around this medium-speed parkland circuit and was full of excitement afterwards, saying: "I was so excited when I drove out of the garage for the first time. It was an incredible feeling as I have

» Lewis could easily have found himself as a test driver in 2007, but Ron Dennis reckoned that he was ready to race in Formula One and he had a vacancy...

"I have wanted to be a Formula One driver since I started in karting and now I am and enjoying every single moment."

Lewis Hamilton

wanted to be an Formula One driver since I started karting and now I am and enjoying every single moment."

Lewis qualified impressively in fourth place, behind only Ferrari's Kimi Raikkonen, team-mate Fernando Alonso and BMW Sauber's Nick Heidfeld, but he instantly made people aware of his uncanny racing skills on the run to the first corner. With the inside line blocked, Lewis jinked to his left and went around the outside of not only Kubica, who had passed him on the run to corner, but Alonso too as they turned into the right-hander. Seasoned onlookers were amazed, their applause instant.

Then, cool as you like, Lewis raced on, being elevated to second place when Heidfeld pitted early. When ace leader Raikkonen pitted four laps earlier than Lewis it left him in the lead. After making his first ever Formula One pit stop in race conditions, Lewis was overhauled by Alonso, while Raikkonen raced on to victory. In taking a podium finish at his first attempt, he was third, Lewis made the best debut since Jacques Villeneuve was second beihind Damon Hill at Albert Park in 1996.

Raikkonen had won on his Ferrari debut, but it was Lewis who the world's press pursued, sure a star had been born. "I'm ecstatic," said Lewis. "Today's result is more than I ever dreamed of achieving on my debut. The race was intense, and I made a few mistakes but nothing major and really enjoyed myself. It was great to lead for a few laps, but I knew it was only temporary. Fernando got past me at the second pit stop as he was able to stay out longer and I lost time behind backmarkers."

Mercedes-Benz motorsport boss Norbert Haug was full of praise: "Lewis made a perfect start to his F1 career and proved absolutely worthy of the confidence we have had in him for the past 10 years."

There were three weeks until the Malaysian GP, in the sapping heat and humidity of Sepang. Here, however, Lewis gave a clear demonstration that his debut had been no fluke, as he braved it out around the outside of Massa at Turn 2 on lap 1, putting himself on the correct line to be ahead of the Ferrari driver as they came out of the corner. Not only did this take balls and precision, it also cemented the fact that this Formula One rookie would bow to no one. Better still for McLaren, it put their cars first and second and enabled Alonso to make good his escape. Lewis motored on to complete a famous one-two as Alonso took his first win for McLaren and Lewis sampled being runner-up for the first time. The occupants of the press room were pleased for Alonso, but their new-found respect for Lewis was palpable.

"That was the toughest race of my career," said Lewis proudly. "It was extremely exhausting defending second place. If you are on your own in the lead you have a

First grand prix, first grand prix podium and the result made the sports world sit up and pay attention.

slightly easier time than you do when you're trying to keep your position, especially when there are two extremely quick Ferraris behind you. At one point, Felipe was attacking at Turn 4 and ended up going off the track. It was extremely intense and by the end I'd run out of drinking water, so it was tough trying to stay ahead of Kimi."

Alonso was delighted, giving Lewis a huge embrace in parc ferme. "To win after coming second in Australia with my new team is like a dream come true," he said.

Team boss Dennis was equally full of praise: "There is a new spirit within the team. Fernando delivers a wealth of experience and racing capability, while Lewis continues to demonstrate why he has warranted the enthusiasm of all of us who have worked with him over the years."

Emphasising the contrast within the world championship calendar, the next stop just one week later was the Bahrain GP at the Sakhir circuit in the scrubby desert. This time around, humidity definitely wasn't going to be a factor in driver fatigue, although the heat was still more than 30 degrees. It was to prove a landmark race, as Lewis outraced Alonso for the first time. He qualified second, behind Massa's Ferrari, and chased the Brazilian all the way to the flag, finishing just 2.2s in arrears. Alonso was fifth, leaving Lewis, himself and Raikkonen atop the championship table.

With a break of four weeks until the Spanish GP, Lewis was champing at the bit to go racing again and it showed in the way that he attacked on the run to the Barcelona circuit's first corner as he passed Raikkonen to climb to third. An instant later, he was second, the position gifted to him by Alonso who was too ambitious in trying to pass pole-starter Massa and ran wide into the Turn 1 gravel, much to the disappointment of the capacity crowd who had come looking for a home win.

Massa again dominated the race, but another second place was enough to put Lewis into the championship lead, on his own. Alonso recovered, but only to third, 10s down, and people wondered if Lewis, rather than Alonso, was McLaren's team leader. Unsurprisingly, this didn't sit well with the reigning world champion.

❝❝Things just keep getting better and I continue living my dream.❞❞

Lewis Hamilton

"Things just keep getting better and I continue living my dream," Lewis effused. "I was struggling to get heat into the tyres in the early stages and had oversteer, but things improved considerably a few laps into the race, although the gap to Felipe was already too big."

Monaco, a fabled street circuit at which Lewis had won in Formula Three and again in GP2, was next and Lewis arrived to a barrage of questions about his relationship with Alonso. Specialist magazine *Autosport's* ran a cover stating "Lewis is number one...but can McLaren handle it?" Asked if the relationship had changed now that he was leading the points table, Lewis replied: "I don't think it's changed. With the team, the relationship grows constantly. I've been at McLaren for a long, long time, and it just gets better and better. We're working extremely hard together to succeed and it's going extremely well at the moment so, as you can see, it's getting better and better. With me and Fernando, the relationship is growing. Off the track, we're friends, we can talk, we're relaxed, there's no tension there."

So, that ghost was laid to rest, but Lewis came away at the end of Sunday afternoon with second place from the race, but the British. press felt that Lewis had been fast enough to win. Perhaps he had but, as he had been running behind Alonso, McLaren urged both of their drivers to ease off. Allegations of McLaren ensuring Alonso beat Lewis don't hold water. lit was common sense that the team didn't want its drivers fighting each other for victory, in case one made a mistake and hit the barriers. Alonso led on merit, so there was no point in asking him to pull aside and no point in leaving Lewis free to potentially put them both off with a failed passing move. The sport's governing body, the FIA, reviewed the race and ruled that all had been fair and just. After all, McLaren hadn't asked a quicker driver to slow down and let his team-mate through, as Ferrari did to boos in the 2002 Austrian GP.

Lewis toed the party line: "To finish second and run similar lap times to Fernando at Monaco makes me very happy. My start was quite good and I ran close to Fernando, but it didn't make sense to try anything crazy. Our job is to ensure maximum points for the team. It's almost impossible to overtake in Monaco and your only chance is for the guy in front to make a mistake. Fernando is a double world champion, so I knew there would be none."

Not surprisingly, Dennis was full of praise for his drivers, especially as they had extended McLaren's lead over Ferrari to 20 points. "Fernando and Lewis responded excellently to the team's wishes of bringing

« He may have been tired, as his drinks bottle had stopped working in the Malaysian heat, but Lewis acknowledges his first second place.

"We've nailed our colours to the mast. There are no holds barred."

Anthony Hamilton

both cars home safely," he said. "However, there is some disappointment because of different strategies we needed to follow to cope with a potential deployment of the Safety Car which has happened four times in the past five years. Once the first round of pitstops had taken place, we reverted Lewis from a one-stop-strategy to the faster two-stop-strategy and slowed both cars to conserve the brakes. We would like to race, but this circuit requires a disciplined approach."

Lewis's maiden win duly came in the Canadian GP at the infamous car-breaker, the Circuit Gilles Villeneuve. Narrow and surrounded by concrete walls, the Montreal circuit is a challenge to every driver, and this was Lewis's first race there, but took pole, beating Alonso, who made an error on his qualifying lap. Alonso tried to pass Lewis at the first corner, got it wrong and fell back to third place behind Heidfeld, leaving Lewis free to do as he pleased. The hardest part of Lewis's run to a maiden victory was the Safety Car being deployed four times. Lewis remained calm through all of these travails to achieve his destiny. His father Anthony was beside himself with joy afterwards as Lewis completed an emotional slowing-down lap and then climbed jubilantly from his silver and dayglo orange racer to head for the podium to lift his first Formula One winner's trophy and then uncork the Champagne.

Dennis was delighted, but kept his pride in check as he commented on Alonso's troubled run to seventh place: "The frustration of Fernando receiving a stop-and-go penalty, having been forced to stop in the pit lane when the pit lane was closed in the first Safety Car period was immense. However, this in no way should detract from a mature and disciplined drive by Lewis to claim his first win. His family should be justifiably proud of his achievement and whatever McLaren and Mercedes-Benz have contributed only compliments his talent and commitment."

Lewis led Alonso by eight points, Massa by 15 and Raikkonen 21, so world title talk grew in momentum. "We can no longer say 'maybe we'll fight for the world championship'." said Anthony, Lewis's dad. "We are going for points and if we get a win that's great. We've nailed our colours to the mast. There are no holds barred."

Next stop was the United States GP at the Indianapolis Motor Speedway, where American fans, including rap artist Pharrell Williams, were fully receptive to Lewismania. America, after all loves a winner and Lewis immediately showed America's Formula One fans exactly why they should love him.

A fly in the ointment, however, was Alonso who felt he was being marginalised in a British team that

» Lewis loves Monaco, but his hopes of victory there in F1 were kept in check when McLaren opted for a safe one-two rather than letting Lewis go for glory.

This hug says it all for Anthony after Lewis scored that first win in Montreal. That was the first ambition claimed...

was fielding a British driver. He was determined to resume control on the track, but Lewis beat him to pole when running with an identical fuel load. Lewis led away at the start, too, held off a high-speed challenge and raced won again, proving himself not only to be ultra-fast and fearless, but resilient too.

Lewis was in seventh heaven: "It keeps getting better and better. I can't believe that I have won and am so incredibly grateful to the team who have worked so hard to continue the development which has seen us taking one-two here. Everything went right; start, pitstops, strategy and I'm really happy. I was under pressure all the way from Fernando and we were pushing as hard as possible. In the second stint, Fernando managed to get really close when my tyres were graining, and he had a go at the end of the straight, but I was able to keep him behind."

Between the United States GP and the French GP, Lewis made a rare appearance in England as the star of the Goodwood Festival of Speed, where he was feted like a hero, interviewed and signed autographs for thousands, all along thinking that if this was Goodwood, what would his welcome be at the British GP.

Lewis was the flavour of the month at Magny-Cours, even though the track suited the Ferrari F2007s, with their longer wheelbases, showing their capabilities around the fast sweeping bends. And so it proved, but only just. A tiny slip by Lewis on his final qualifying lap meant he split the Ferraris on the grid, but then a poor getaway saw him demoted to third by Raikkonen. Lewis was hemmed in behind the Finn, allowing Massa to pull away. He could do nothing to elevate his position. A short-fuel second stop, putting him on to a three-stop run, resulted in Lewis being passed by Kubica's BMW Sauber as he rejoined. The Pole also had a stop to make, but Lewis couldn't afford to be delayed and so pulled off one of the moves of the season when he outbraked him into the Adelaide hairpin. It was a blinder of a move and he duly raced on to that third place to extend his championship lead to 14 points over Alonso who fought bravely to move from tenth at the start to seventh at the flag.

"I didn't have the best start and I don't know exactly what the reason was," said Lewis. "My car was very good in the opening stage of the race, and I pushed hard to get past Kimi, but it didn't work out, so we opted for a three-stop strategy."

Dennis explained the change of tactics: "We had the option of switching between a two or three-stop strategy for Lewis, and we opted for the latter to ensure that he had minimal traffic and maintained his strong and safe third position."

Asked post-race about the thrill of heading to his home race with a 14-point lead, Lewis replied: "I am very happy with the job that I have done and the job that the

 The pressure from Alonso was intense, but Lewis weathered the storm and victory in the US GP made it two on the trot.

"Going into my first British GP leading the championship is one of the greatest feelings."

Lewis Hamilton

team have done and I think that going into my first British GP with the team that I have always wanted to drive for and leading the world championship is one of the greatest feelings that a driver can have."

On the Friday, the first day of the meeting. Lewis was fast, but the Ferraris were faster. watched by a record crowd of 42,000 who felt sure that Ferrari wouldn't waltz away as they had at Magny-Cours. By Saturday, Lewis had charmed double that number to attend qualifying (a record for a British GP Saturday crowd) and snatched pole at the death. Father, Anthony, jigged in the pit lane and the packed grandstands erupted. They were all living the dream. But there was a dark cloud on the horizon, the espionage story centred on McLaren chief designer Mike Coughlan.

Race day wasn't as kind and, after a mistake at his first pit stop, when Lewis tried to leave before the fuel hose had been disengaged, the lead was taken by Alonso. Then, after the second round of stops, it was Ferrari's Raikkonen in control as Lewis dropped ever further back in third. Yet, when the hubbub subsided, McLaren could reflect on their decision a few weeks earlier to keep Lewis away from the pre-British GP tests at Silverstone. Maybe those extra laps might have made a difference.

"I got a good start and tried to pull out a gap, but Kimi was extremely quick," explained Lewis. "Unfortunately, I made a mistake in the pit stop, which cost me a few seconds. I was more consistent towards the end, but the team chose to save the engine for the Nurburgring. The fans have been tremendous, and the race would have been harder without their support."

Dennis was sanguine about being beaten by Ferrari for the second race in a row: "Fernando did a tremendous job, making every effort to turn our short-fuel middle stint into a win. Ultimately, he and Lewis were asked to turn their engines down to ensure that we had the best ability to attack again in Germany."

The European GP at the Nurburgring was next, and Lewis needed to re-establish himself after Raikkonen's back-to-back wins. Fortunately the circuit's layout, with more medium-speed twists and turns and fewer high-speed turns, were better suited to the McLaren. and Lewis had dominated the GP2 races there in 2006.

He was still able to top the timesheets in the first of Friday's practice sessions and be faster than all but Raikkonen in the afternoon. He was second behind the Finn again on the Saturday morning, but the images beamed around the world on the Saturday afternoon caused Lewis fans to gasp, for there was their hero mounting the kerbs early in final qualifiying, skipping across a gravel bed and slamming into the tyre wall at 150mph. It was a while until the rescue crew released him from the cockpit.

" The race would have been harder without the fans' support. "

Lewis Hamilton

By then, the replays had shown that the accident wasn't Lewis' fault, as his right front wheel had come loose and its tyre was cut, deflating suddenly. Dennis confirmed that this was down to a fault with the wheelgun. He remained clearly worried, despite a winded Lewis having shown a thumbs-up as he was stretchered into the ambulance, as he had had no further news. Lewis was just shaken so, if he was cleared to race, his title aspirations were still on, although he would start from 10th on the grid.

It was dry as Raikkonen accelerated away from pole, but Lewis had passed four cars by the first corner. Out of Turn 2, he was up to fourth after the BMWs tangled, but he'd clipped one when it spun and picked up a puncture. Rain hit as he had a slow drive back to the pits, during which the downpour had transformed Turn 1 into a lake and, even on rain tyres, he joined car after car that had aquaplaned off there. The difference was, Lewis kept his engine going and was craned out, losing a lap, but able to take the restart.

Lewis drove like a demon in pursuit of points. The rain returned in the final few laps, and Lewis missed out on scoring by 1.5s, having passed Giancarlo Fisichella a lap from home and closed in on Heikki Kovalainen. At least McLaren ended up with a winner, with Alonso barging his way past Massa five laps from home. Lewis's points lead over Alonso was down to only two.

What Lewis needed after the European GP was to regain momentum. What McLaren needed was to put the spying allegations behind them and get back to racing at the Hungarian GP.

Lewis achieved the former, but neither escaped the world of intrigue after a bizarre third qualifying session in which Lewis was delayed in the pits by Alonso to the extent that he didn't have enough time to get back onto the track to complete his final flying lap before the chequered flag fell at the end of the session, offering him no opportunity to regain pole after his team-mate snatched it from him. The

Felipe Massa lines up on pole position at Magny-Cours, but Lewis, in second grid position, would soon lose ground.

incident was investigated by the stewards, who took almost until midnight to decide on their response: they charged Alonso with impeding an opponent and moved him back from first to sixth.

Lewis was elevated to pole and moved from the dirty side of the grid. A good start was imperative, particularly on a circuit where overtaking is so hard to do. Nick Heidfeld's BMW Sauber was on the outside of the front row, but the usually fast-starting German was not Lewis's equal, and he also lost out to Raikkonen.

What followed was a dogfight that lasted all the way to the chequered flag. There were occasions when Raikkonen was right on his tail, with Lewis troubled in his second stint by a steering wheel that was angled to the right, but he took the gap out from 1s to 4.4s thanks to a handful of quick laps when he stayed out four laps longer before making his final pit stop. But then Raikkonen banged in a series of laps that were fully 1s faster than Lewis and was back on his tail. Now was the time for Lewis to dig deep, keep his cool and refrain from a slip, something that wasn't always easy when negotiating traffic. Takuma Sato gave Lewis a particular scare when he emerged from the pits into his path at Turn 1. Lewis was pumped up, his determination to win greater than ever after the perceived lack of fairness in qualifying and he tied it all up for his third win from 11 starts. With Alonso delayed by Ralf Schumacher in the early laps and unable to pass Heidfeld for third, Lewis stretched his points advantage from two points to seven.

After the trials and tribulations of Hungary and a break of two weekends, it was back into action for Lewis and the gang at the Turkish GP at the end of August. The media, given so much opportunity to fan the flames at the Hungaroring, were keen to follow up on the antagonism between Lewis and Fernando, but after a team meeting to clear the air on the Thursday neither driver offered them much succour.

On the track, though, there was a more immediate enemy: Ferrari. Indeed, McLaren had feared that the Italian team would have the upper hand around the fast, open curves of the Istanbul circuit and so it proved as Massa took pole. It was incredibly close, though, with Lewis lapping just 0.044s slower to line up second ahead of Raikkonen and Alonso. In fact, Lewis had carried an extra lap of fuel too, so a different gamble could have seen him starting from pole. He would then have had both track position and the clean side of the circuit at the start. Instead, Raikkonen shot past Lewis before Turn 1 and there was nothing that he could do to overturn the deficit in those two laps between Massa pitting from the lead and Lewis coming in for his first stop.

"I guess these things happen when you fight for the championship."

Lewis Hamilton

Lewis's hopes of being best of the rest behind the Ferraris went awry when his right front tyre blew at Turn 9 of lap 43, three laps before his second pit stop was due. He limped back to the pits and rejoined the race in fifth place, behind Alonso and Heidfeld, and held the position to the end to collect four points.

By the time of the Italian GP, intra-team troubles had quelled, but the spectre of the FIA's World Motor Sport Council making judgment on spying charges against the team on the Thursday after the race left McLaren less than chirpy. The team response was to beat Ferrari on home ground. They locked out the front row, with Alonso beating Lewis for pole. Lewis had to get in front at the start if he was to control the race. His bid for the lead was compromised, as he explains: "I didn't get the best getaway and Felipe managed to shoot past me. I outbraked both him and Fernando into Turn 1, and I almost thought I was going to get past, but then Felipe clipped me and sent me over the second part of the chicane."

Before the lap was out, though, the safety car had been deployed as David Coulthard had crashed at Curva Grande following contact at the first chicane with Giancarlo Fisichella. Lewis had a second chance to try and overtake Alonso. It didn't work and Alonso eased clear from there. Massa retired, so only Raikkonen could topple the McLarens. He ran a one-stop strategy, and though slower than Lewis and Alonso, he saved the 22s needed for that second stop. Lewis fell to third behind Raikkonen after his second stop but got his place back with a stunning move at the first chicane three laps later. Alonso was now three points behind Lewis.

Before Formula One's return to Spa-Francorchamps, McLaren was stripped of its Constructors' Cup points for the whole season by the governing body, effectively handing Ferrari the trophy. The team fine of $100m left all of motor racing reeling.

Spa suited the Ferraris more than the McLarens as Raikkonen claimed pole, ahead of Massa, Alonso and Lewis. Raikkonen won, but at the first corner Alonso forced Lewis wide out of the hairpin after being bunched by Massa and had to back off to avoid a collision. But he swung to the outside kerb and pushed Lewis onto the run-off area. "I got a good start and thought I had a chance to get past," said Lewis, "but I had to run wide as Fernando kept to the inside. I guess these things happen when you fight for the championship."

Lewis wasn't about to give up, and was alongside as they accelerated down the hill towards Eau Rouge. Lewis braved it out side-by-side through the left-hand part before opting for safety over possible glory. It was clear that Ferrari's straightline speed was too much for the McLarens and they pulled away, with Massa unable to

⮝ This is what happens when you have a tyre deflate at 150mph, going into a corner, as Lewis discovered in the final qualifying session at the Nurburgring.

match Raikkonen. By flagfall, Alonso was 10s behind Massa, with Lewis a further 9s adrift. Lewis's lead was cut to two points over Alonso, while Raikkonen's victory moved him to within 13 points, so the battle was really hotting up.

When people look back over 2007, Lewis's Japanese GP will shine out. On the sideslopes of Japan's Mount Fuji, he displayed a James Bond-like cool to win a race run in extreme conditions. Lewis was the man in qualifying, by only 0.07s, but it grew in importance when the track was shrouded in fog on race day and streaked with rain. The race went for 19 laps behind the safety car, but the risk of aquaplaning remained.

The Ferraris were soon out of the reckoning, having not started on extreme wets, so Lewis had only Alonso as a rival. It all could have gone wrong on lap 34 when Kubica hit Lewis. "I didn't see him coming," said Lewis, "so the impact caught me by surprise, and I spun." This dropped him behind Kovalainen, but he was back in the lead five laps later when the Finn pitted and the pressure eased on lap 43 when Alonso crashed, stretching his points advantage to 12, with Raikkonen 17 behind, his outside chance continuing after scrabbling his way back to third behind Kovalainen after Vettel knocked Webber out of second.

Lewis was delighted, but he wasn't celebrating: "This was an important win, but I don't want to think too much about it and will focus on the Chinese GP."

After practice in Shanghai, Lewis appeared to be third or fourth fastest. Yet, after qualifying, Alonso was kicking doors in the McLaren HQ after Lewis grabbed pole. Then, under leaden skies, Lewis made a perfect start. Raikkonen was safe in second, but Alonso passed Massa as they exited Turn 2 before a slow exit from Turn 3 enabled Massa to regain third. Lewis was 0.7s clear at the end of lap 1 and going away. On the pit wall, all eyes were on the sky as rain blew in.

Lewis was the first to pit, on lap 15 from an 8.6s lead, but only for fuel as he kept on his intermediates. He re-emerged in fourth ahead of Coulthard. The key would be how much longer Raikkonen would run and he set a series of fastest laps before stopping on lap 19. The gap came down to 4s. What followed was perplexing as Raikkonen made his first attack on lap 28, Lewis fought to hold him off. Why? All he needed was eight points and this was with Alonso winning, not Raikkonen.

Raikkonen took the lead on lap 29 when Lewis slid wide. Dry tyres were now the ones to have as Wurz had had them fitted and was lapping fastest. It was up to the

" "I'm pretty disappointed ... However, this is only my first year in F1 and overall it has been phenomenal."**""**

Lewis Hamilton

teams to read the changing conditions, and McLaren were to leave him out too long on tyres that were shot, the canvas visible on the left rear. When Lewis pitted on lap 31, he ran wide and his car became stuck in a gravel trap. His only hope was that the win wouldn't go to closest rival Alonso who had closed onto his tail. Raikkonen won, with Alonso and Massa taking the minor places.

Lewis stormed off. A while later, he talked to the press in an amazingly upbeat manner, saying: "Don't worry, there's a race to go, so I can still do it."

In Brazil, the message was still beamed out that everything was going to be fine. Then rain fell and the Ferraris were faster. Yet Lewis learned Interlagos in a flash and was fastest when it dried.

In qualifying, Massa went top, but Lewis slotted in a stunning middle section on his final flier and was ahead going into the long final corner. He just missed pole, but his lap was good enough for second on the grid and, perhaps most importantly, Alonso would start two places further back, behind Raikkonen. That just left the race...

Losing a place to Raikkonen wasn't a disaster, but the Finn tripped over Massa and had to lift off. Lewis did too to avoid him and this let Alonso have a run into Turn 3 and get past. Lewis then lost his cool in his desire to get back into third, locked up and ran off the track. He rejoined eighth, with a mountain to climb. On lap 8, his McLaren slowed and 30s were lost before it got up to speed again as a gear-shifting problem was fixed with advice radioed from the pits. Eighth had become 18th.

Lewis had to start overtaking, even passing four cars on one lap. Webber retiring from fifth handed him another place, so Lewis was up to 10th when he pitted for the second time, but it was only for a short-fuel. The team fitted the softer rubber. He then pressed like mad, with a heart-in-mouth moment when he dived inside Barrichello's Honda. Alonso could not keep up with the Ferraris and was being troubled by Kubica.

Having risen to eighth by lap 56, Lewis's third pitstop ended his chance to catch Heidfeld and work his way towards the fifth place he needed with Raikkonen leading the race. He got back one place when Trulli pitted, but that was it. Kubica and Rosberg's battle might have led to a collision, but they didn't and seventh was all he could manage, leaving the tally at 110 points for Raikkonen, 109 for Lewis and Alonso.

There was disappointment but also pride, and the final words on a season that so nearly produced the first world title for a rookie ought to go to Lewis: "I am disappointed, having led for so much of the season and then not to win the championship. However, this is only my first year in F1 and it has been phenomenal. I am still young and have plenty more years to achieve my dream."

Alonso leads Lewis in a McLaren one-two ahead of the Ferraris in the early laps of the Italian GP on a weekend when F1 needed sport to come to the fore.

3. **THE FORMULA ONE SEASON 2008**

THE FORMULA ONE SEASON 2008

The winter went by in a flash and by March it was time to go again. As ever, the mix was different, with Alonso having returned to Renault, swapping rides with Kovalainen. The matter of who would be top dog at McLaren wasn't discussed, but Lewis was seen as team leader and this was how it shaped out through the first half of the season.

After all the acrimony of 2007, McLaren simply wanted to go racing in Australia. Pole position for Lewis was the start they craved, with Kovalainen a competitive third. Then came the ultimate fillip, as Lewis kept his cool through three safety car periods to give his second title bid the best start possible. Better still, neither Ferrari driver scored, with the podium completed by BMW Sauber's Heidfeld and Williams racer Rosberg. If Lewis was feeling vindictive, he might have smiled at Alonso qualifying 11th, although Alonso advanced to fourth, albeit fourth out of only seven finishers.

"What a dream start," beamed Lewis. "We were quite close into the first corner, but I was able to pull a good gap at the exit and just had to look after the tyres from then on. I'm sorry not to have Heikki with me on the podium, as a one-two would have been a great reward to the team. It's nice to have Nico [Rosberg] here though, as we haven't shared a podium since our karting days. I controlled the race, but we had to change our strategy constantly and the strategists were on the ball throughout."

The Malaysian GP was next, just one week later, and the pendulum swung the other way, towards Ferrari. What made the gap larger still in the race is that Lewis and Kovalainen were given five-place grid penalties for impeding rivals' flying laps as they made their fuel-saving in-lap at the end of qualifying. This left them eighth and ninth respectively. To add to Lewis's woes, his charge to fourth place was wrecked at his first pit stop when he lost 10s when a wheel nut-locking mechanism failed. This left him to finish fifth, a whacking 46s behind race winner Raikkonen, with Kubica showing BMW Sauber's progress with second place.

"I got a really good start and was pretty happy as we jumped from ninth to fifth," explained Lewis. "I was pushing Mark [Webber] for a long time, but being behind someone, no matter how quick you are, it's difficult to get past. We were in a good position for a shot at third." Then came the pit stop blunder.

The humidity of Malaysia was swapped for the dry heat of Bahrain and Lewis came away with nothing. Having qualified third behind Kubica – who everyone reckoned had qualified with a light fuel load and would thus be pitting early – and Massa, Lewis made a mess of blasting off at the start, losing six places by the first corner.

» Back to winning ways. Lewis Hamilton put behind him the disappointment of last year with the perfect start to the 2008 World Championship – a win in Australia.

Lewis gives his crew the thumbs-up after bouncing back to finish third in Spain after the disappointments of Sepang.

Then, in his fightback, Lewis rode over the back of Alonso's Renault, enforcing a stop for repairs, dropping him to 18th, from which he could regain only five places. To add to his upset, it was a Ferrari one-two, led by Massa, with Kubica and team-mate Heidfeld competitive in third and fourth, and Kovalainen some way back in fifth, so it was plain that the title battle would be between three teams and thus six drivers. Full of disappointment, Lewis said: "I let the team down. I messed up at the start as I didn't hit the switch early enough and hadn't engaged the correct engine setting. The anti-stall kicked in and I lost a lot of places, but things were salvageable. Then I was behind Fernando and moved to the right, and he moved to the right and that was it."

Lewis's lack of pace in the second half of the race came more from the heavy fuel load he was carrying after being put onto a one-stop strategy, as team chief Ron Dennis explained: "After Lewis's bad start and the incident with Fernando which hampered his pace, we took the decision to save the engine for the next race."

Lewis was back on the podium at that next race, in Barcelona, but McLaren had been given a major fright. This wasn't so much down to Ferrari's strong pace, but due to Kovalainen having a huge accident at Campsa corner from which he was fortunate to escape with just a stiff neck after a 145mph impact following wheel failure.

Raikkonen was in peerless form and dominated from pole, but Lewis gave it his all to finish third, starting off by outwitting Kubica into Turn 1, then taking third from Alonso when he pitted early for fuel as a result of showboating in qualifying for his home grand prix. There was nothing that he could do to usurp the Ferraris and so third it was, 4.1s behind Raikkonen.

Climbing out of his car, Lewis's first response was to ask about his team-mate: "I saw a car had gone into the barriers and was told it was Heikki. As soon as the team knew he was OK, Ron radioed and told me."

Not surprisingly, Dennis's concerns were focused on why one of his cars had crashed: "Our data shows evidence of a sudden tyre deflation, but it's too early to identify what triggered that deflation although it's likely to have been the result of a wheel rim failure."

“I am thrilled. It's not about winning, it's about feeling that you extract 100% from yourself and the car.”

Lewis Hamilton

With four wins to his name in his maiden season of Formula 1, and another at the start of 2008, you would have been surprised that Lewis was so excited after finishing second in the Turkish GP, but he even described it as "the best race I've ever done."

Why so? Because he had to adapt to a three-stop strategy to make his front right tyres last around the Istanbul Park circuit, particularly as a failure in 2007 scuppered his race. So it was that, starting third on the grid behind Massa and Kovalainen, who was back to full strength, Lewis had to maximise every lap. He grabbed second at the start as Kovalainen struggled to get away from the dirty side of the grid and then was hit by Raikkonen and picked up a puncture. From there, Lewis had not only to catch Massa, but pass him, which he managed into Turn 12 on lap 24 and then pulled out a second per lap on each of the nine laps before his second stop. His pace was sufficient to overhaul Raikkonen but not Massa and by flagfall, the gap was 3.7s.

Lewis was exultant: "I am thrilled. It's not about winning, it's about feeling that you extract 100% from yourself and the car. Before the race, our prediction was that I would finish fifth. I reckon if I had managed to get the car on pole, I could have won."

Mercedes motorsport boss Norbert Haug revealed the racer within when he picked out Lewis's pass on Massa: "His manoeuvre when he passed Massa was surely enjoyed by millions of television spectators as it does not happen too often in Formula 1 that the leading car is passed."

The joy continued at Monaco where not only did Lewis win, but he moved into the championship lead. This was no straightforward win, as conditions were treacherous, there were incidents aplenty and, oh yes, Lewis collected two punctures on the way…

Pole position is the place to start at this circuit. Lewis qualified third but passed Raikkonen by the first corner, Ste Devote. Massa's Ferrari blinded him with its spray, then on lap 5 Lewis slid into the barrier at Tabac. The resultant puncture could have been a disaster, but McLaren reacted in a flash, were ready for him and put in enough fuel to take him past halfway and he came back out in fifth, such was the amount that the field had strung out on the wet track. Then out came the safety car after Coulthard hit the barriers at Massenet and was hit by Bourdais' Toro Rosso, letting Lewis close right up, having taken fourth when Alonso also hit the barriers. Then Raikkonen pitted for a drive-through penalty, putting Lewis third. A dozen laps later, this became second when Kubica made his first stop from a lead he'd gained when Massa went up an escape road. On lap 33 of 76, Lewis took the lead when Massa pitted.

The drivers' main concern was whether it was going to rain again, giving them options to get it wrong on the timing of their stops and tyre choice. For Lewis, fuelled heavy, there was flexibility, but he didn't need it and won as he pleased from Kubica and Massa, then picked up a second puncture on the slowing down lap…

"I'm over the moon," gushed Lewis. "To win in Monaco is the highlight of my career. There was a lot of water on the track at Tabac, and suddenly I had oversteer. We changed our strategy, and I had to make only one more stop. When I was 40s ahead, the team told me to take it easy." Dennis was full of admiration: "Our guys instigated a brilliant strategy change, under pressure, after Lewis touched the barrier. Had Heikki not had a problem on the grid, we'd have had the pace for a one-two."

Montreal, scene of his maiden win in 2007, could easily have yielded a repeat performance, yet the all but inevitable deployment of the safety car changed not only the course of his race, but potentially his championship. It came out on lap 17 after Adrian Sutil had his Force India fail and it was decided to remove it from the side of the track. As soon as the pit lane was opened, the bunched field dived in and Kubica and Raikkonen got back on their way faster. The red light greeted them at pit exit, so they stopped. Head down behind them, Lewis failed to stop in time and slammed into Raikkonen, taking both out of the race, with Rosberg sliding into his tail before continuing.

In a flash, not only had Lewis – by far the fastest in the race – lost the race, but he was later given a 10-place grid penalty for the next race. It was a calamity and made all the worse when a maiden win for Kubica moved him to the head of the points table.

"Before my pit stop, everything looked on course for the perfect result," said Lewis. "We were breezing it. But as I exited the box, I saw two cars jostling for position ahead of me. Obviously, I didn't want to get involved in their tussle, and was trying not to do so, and then all of a sudden they stopped. It's just unfortunate when stuff like this happens." Many felt he underplayed his disappointment. After all, this was the loss of many points, with further damage to come in the next race, and this from a man who missed out in 2007 by just one point.

If it was expected that the French GP would offer up a limited yield of points, Lewis and McLaren must have expected at least some. But Lewis came away empty-handed, and was now 10 points adrift of race winner Massa who moved back to the top of the points table as Lewis fell to fourth.

Third place in qualifying became 13th when his 10-place grid penalty from Canada was applied. Lewis had a real go at undoing some of the damage on the first lap, and

"He demonstrated that he's unquestionably the best wet-weather driver of his generation."

Sir Jackie Stewart

passed Heidfeld and Coulthard then got past Vettel at the Nurburgring esse. Trouble was, he was adjudged to have cut the corner and was given a drive-through penalty. This was a double disaster and put Lewis back to 13th and he was not to climb back any higher than 10th. At least Kovalainen claimed fourth for the team behind Massa, Raikkonen and Toyota's Jarno Trulli.

Lewis was nonplussed: "My drive-through was an extremely close call. I felt I'd got past Vettel fairly and was ahead going into the corner. But I was on the outside and couldn't turn-in in case we crashed, then I lost the back-end and drove over the kerb."

After examining the data, Haug summed up the team's frustration best, saying: "Without his drive-through, third place would definitely have been possible for Lewis."

The most important thing, as stumbling politicians always seem to say, was to draw a line under the matter. And Lewis did this in considerable style at the British GP.

Team-mate Kovalainen claimed his first pole and this will have rankled Lewis, not because he doesn't like him, but because it should have been him at the top of the time sheets. The problem was, he ran wide through the gravel towards the end of what would have been his best lap and was cautious on the follow-up, ending up fourth.

Lewis mastered the getaway on a wet track so well that he was vying with Kovalainen for the lead by the first corner. What followed, as his rivals spun here, there and everywhere, was a masterful drive, with Lewis ducking out of Kovalainen's spray to take the lead at Stowe on lap 5. Then, with the track drying, Raikkonen passed Kovalainen and closed right in on Lewis. They pitted together, but Ferrari left Raikkonen on his used intermediate tyres which proved a mistake as rain returned and Lewis pulled out 21s on him in just five laps. Heavier rain hit just past mid-distance and Lewis simply stretched his lead further, albeit with one off-track moment at Abbey and he went on to win from Heidfeld by the staggering margin of a minute and more, with Raikkonen a lap down in fourth.

Three-time world champion Sir Jackie Stewart paid homage: "He's demonstrated that he's unquestionably the best wet-weather driver of his generation."

Lewis simply said: "It's by far the best victory I've ever had. It was so extreme and slippery out there, very similar to Fuji last year, added to which I was having problems with my visor fogging up. When I came round the last time, I saw the crowd standing up and I prayed: 'just finish, just finish.' It was a very emotional moment to win my home grand prix."

There was a three-way battle between Lewis and the Ferrari drivers when they arrived at Hockenheim for the German GP, with Kubica just two points behind. But

There was much to smile about in 2008, but the Ferrari drivers and BMW Sauber's Robert Kubica kept the pressure on.

then, proving that he was the one with the momentum, Lewis flew out on the Sunday evening four points clear of Massa after a second mighty drive in a row.

Lewis led away from pole and was in total control of the race, pulling out an 11s lead before his first pit stop and then streaking clear of Massa all over again when they had all pitted. There had been considerable aerodynamic development of the McLaren MP4-23 and he was making the most of the changes, while Kovalainen in third, was struggling. But then, at mid-distance, Glock's Toyota slammed into the pit wall, scattering debris and bringing out the safety car. In a flash, Lewis's 12s advantage was wiped out. On the lap that the pit lane reopened, all the frontrunners came in for what would be their final pit stop. All except Lewis. Team supremo Dennis had to hold his hand up for that one: "We decided that, as Lewis still had quite a lot of fuel on board, we would leave him out until lap 50. We'd expected the track to be cleared faster than it was, which would have allowed the safety car to come in earlier. He responded majestically, though."

Indeed he did, as he moved up to warp-speed for the eight laps after the safety car withdrew as he tried to gain the 23s gap he required so that he could come back out in front. As it was, he rejoined in fifth. Kovalainen moved over after a lap. Fourth became third when Heidfeld pitted two laps later and so Massa was his next target. So fast was Lewis, that Massa had no defence into the hairpin. That just left Nelson Piquet Jr, the Renault driver who had found himself at the front by dint of making his one stop just as the safety car came out. He was dispatched at the same corner three laps later and Lewis proved that he was the man, poor pit calls or not. "I would have much preferred an easy afternoon, but it didn't work out that way," quipped Lewis.

Hungary held both good memories for Lewis and bad after his contretemps with Alonso in 2007 was followed by victory. Twelve months later, it was also a case of good news and bad. The good news came first, with another pole position. The bad news came next, when Massa drove around the outside of him at the first corner to take the lead. Then Lewis was not able to strike back. He appeared to have no answers in either the first stint or the second.

Worse was to follow as Lewis suddenly slowed at the start of his 41st lap, his front left tyre punctured. A minute was lost as he limped back to the pits, second place having turned into 10th by the time he rejoined. Immediately, he started chasing after whatever few points he could recover and Lewis was up to sixth with three laps to go when Massa's engine failed, handing Kovalainen his first win and stretching Lewis's points lead to five over Raikkonen who came home third after failing to overhaul Glock.

Delighted at the turn of events, Lewis was relieved: "I felt comfortable in the second stint as I was matching Massa's times but was going to be running longer to the final stops. I could have had a go at passing him, but the damaged tyre stopped that."

The 12th stop on the 18-race tour was at the first of the year's new venues, the Valencia street circuit for the European GP. Infuriatingly, Lewis was in no mood to enjoy the surroundings, as he was suffering from a fever and a neck spasm. However, he had a pain-killing injection and knuckled down to qualify second fastest. Ominously, though, the driver who had shown him the way in Hungary, Massa, was 0.2s faster and carried that advantage into the race, staying ahead into the first corner and pulling away from there. All Lewis could do was keep Kubica behind him and hold on to second, which he did with ease. Massa was as dominant here as Lewis had been at Hockenheim, with Ferrari's advantage being its speed down the straights.

Massa duly racked up the fourth win of his campaign – matching Lewis's tally – but he was adjudged fortunate not to pick up a worse penalty for being flagged out into Sutil's path in the pit lane. Ferrari was fined €10,000 rather than being hit with a drive-through penalty that would have gifted the race to Lewis. In fact, it was a troubled time in the pits for Ferrari, as an out-of-sorts Raikkonen tipped one of his pit crew over and compounded his problems when he lost the chance of any points when his engine blew, and so dropped back to 13 points behind Lewis in the title race.

Dennis knew that Lewis had been roundly beaten, but still found a positive to take away: "We lost the chance of outright victory in qualifying. If Lewis had qualified with the same level of fuel as Felipe, he'd probably have been able to control the race from the front. But the nature of the circuit dictated that it was always going to be difficult for him to overtake."

Looking forward to the Belgian GP with a six-point lead, Lewis felt confident, even though Ferrari had an enviable record at Spa-Francorchamps. What no one could have predicted was what a firecracker of a race it would be.

Leading from pole, Lewis half spun at La Source at the start of lap 2 on the damp track. Although he got going again before Raikkonen arrived in second place, the

"I came out of the second apex in front of Kimi, and so I lifted-off to ensure he got back in front."

Lewis Hamilton

Ferrari driver had more momentum and took the lead after diving out of Lewis's tow up the hill to Les Combes. And that was how it stayed through the two sets of pit stops, but Lewis started to reel him in after changing to the harder tyres. Light rain fell with just three laps to go and Raikkonen struggled under braking. Lewis got partly ahead into the chicane, then was pushed wide by the Finn and left with little option but to go over the kerbs in avoidance.

What followed was contentious, as he emerged in front, backed off and ducked behind Raikkonen, then promptly outbraked him into the hairpin. They tussled again later in the lap, then Raikkonen crashed and Lewis won, describing it as one of the most exciting races of his career. Ron Dennis called it a "sensational grand prix." Their joy was shortlived, though, as the FIA hit him with a 25s penalty, handing victory to Massa who had never been in the reckoning and dropping Lewis to third behind Heidfeld. McLaren's appeal was later rejected.

Lewis was perplexed: "I came out of the second apex in front of Kimi and so I lifted-off to ensure that he got back in front. The team came on the radio and instructed me to allow Kimi to repass, which I'd already done. As a result, he crossed the start/finish line ahead of me and 6.7km/h quicker than me."

Martin Whitmarsh was nonplussed: "We asked Race Control to confirm that they were comfortable that Lewis had allowed Kimi to repass, and they confirmed twice that they believed that the position had been given back in a manner that was OK."

Two triple world champions leapt to Lewis's defence. Niki Lauda called it "the worst decision in motor racing history." Jackie Stewart said: "Raikkonen behaved robustly to defend his position and left Hamilton with no option but to miss the chicane."

When the teams arrived at Monza four days later, the appeal hearing was still four days away, so all they could do was focus on the racing. Or, actually, simply on seeing where they were going, as it rained every day and conditions were treacherous.

The team then slipped up in Q2 by opting for intermediate tyres. The rain didn't ease, though, and Lewis floundered around slowest, to qualify 15th. Massa was sixth and fortunately wasn't able to work his way forward to win. In fact, Lewis did a better job and if the team had stayed as bold as they had been in qualifying and put him on to intermediates at his first stop, he might have been able to improve his position. But they didn't and first-time polesitter Vettel became F1's youngest winner, at just 21, also giving Scuderia Toro Rosso its first win as he headed Heikki home. Massa was able to finish only sixth, one place ahead of Lewis, and so the gap came down to a point.

"If it had kept on raining," said Lewis, "I feel confident I could have won from 15th;

↟ Lewis receives a hug from his father Antony following the Japanese Grand Prix. It was a difficult race for Hamilton who incurared a drivethrough penalty and was bumped by Massa which led to 12th place finish.

↞ After starting fifteenth on the grid in initially rainswept conditions, Lewis finished seventh at Monza. Although disappointing by his own high standards, only one point was relinquished to Felipe Massa in the Drivers' Championship.

but, as the circuit dried out, my tyres overcooked."

Dennis also felt their luck could have been better: "Lewis could have recorded a podium finish had the rain persisted and had he therefore been able to maintain his one-stop strategy. As it was, he was forced to make an unscheduled stop in order to exchange his extreme-wet tyres for wet-weather tyres."

The Singapore GP was a step into a brave new world, not only for its city centre location, but the fact that it was F1's first night race and everyone loved it. Lewis looked to be loving it all the more as he took pole as the flag fell at the end of qualifying. However, Massa had just started his final flier and bagged pole by a large margin.

Fears that this race might follow the pattern of the European GP were being realised when the safety car had to be deployed after Nelson Piquet Jr crashed. If this move had been orchestrated by Renault, it couldn't have worked better, as Alonso had had a mechanical failure in Q2 and was running a very short first stint on the unfavoured soft tyres. In fact, he'd just pitted and now everyone else was backed up behind the safety car. Lewis, who had been second behind Massa when it came out, could only pit when the pits were declared open again and was eighth when the safety car withdrew, albeit behind several cars that were yet to pit. Worse was to befall Massa, as he pulled his refuelling hose with him. However, there was nothing that Lewis could do to get back on terms with Alonso. There was a chance that he might wrest second from Rosberg, though. "After the second re-start, I tried to stay as close as possible behind Nico," explained Lewis, "but I didn't want to take chances – particularly as Ferrari was outside the points." Indeed, Ron Dennis told him not to: "Having seen Kimi's accident, we advised Lewis not to attempt to overtake Nico but instead to settle for a seven-point lead in the Drivers' Championship."

All the talk ahead of the Japanese GP was how Lewis was going to take no risks in gathering points for his title challenge. There was a storm pre-race when Kubica said that many drivers considered Lewis to be too aggressive. Lewis fended this off by saying "I do my talking on the track, so I haven't really got much to say to it."

"I braked a bit late – but so did everybody. A lot of cars went wide at Turn 1 – and I went a bit wider than everybody else."

Lewis Hamilton

Trouble was, a tardy getaway let Raikkonen power into the lead and Lewis reckoned he could take the lead back into Turn 1. He locked up as he dived up the inside and went straight on as he fought to get his car to turn in. Most of the field struggled to get grip on cold tyres, but Lewis struggled the most as he'd braked the latest. Kubica, who started sixth and wasn't caught up in this bunch, was able to take the lead.

Lewis explained what happened: "I braked a bit late – but so did everybody. A lot of cars went wide at Turn 1 – and I went a bit wider than everyone else."

Lewis didn't need to pass Raikkonen. His focus had to be Massa who had started fifth. Lewis's attack attracted criticism for not considering the bigger picture. Among the critics was Sir Jackie Stewart who said: "There's an adage that 'you can't win the race in the first corner, but you can lose it'. I suspect that Lewis, despite all his calmness out of the cockpit, did not carry out his (and McLaren's) gameplan."

Lewis was later to be given a drivethrough penalty. But, even before he was hit with that, something else hit him: Massa. This was at Turn 11, when the Ferrari driver braked late for the first part of the chicane and Lewis slipped by, only for Massa to run across the grass and pitch him into a spin. By the time he'd recovered, Lewis was last but one. Massa was also given a drivethrough. To make matters worse, with Lewis finishing 12th, Massa came eighth and was boosted to seventh when Bourdais was penalized 25s for being hit by Massa rather than vice versa.

Ron Dennis was philosophical, although no doubt wishing that Lewis had exerted caution: "We were surprised that Lewis was given a penalty. Drivers miss braking points, they run wide; these things happen."

So, the gap was down to five points but proof that Lewis's focus was total in China came when he was fastest in Friday's practice sessions, then secured pole with aplomb. That just the left the race. Or, more importantly, the run to the first corner. Only then could Dennis heave a sigh of relief as Lewis was easily in front. The outside chance of rain eased and there were no repeats of the tyre fiasco of 2007. Massa was waved through for second by Raikkonen towards the end. The race belonged to only one person, though: Lewis.

"Everything went right," beamed Lewis. "I made one of my best-ever starts and had perfect balance during the race. I owe so much of that to the guys in the team as they did an amazing job. It might be another step towards my dream, but we've got to keep our heads."

And so to Brazil for the shoot-out. Massa simply had to take pole and did, with Lewis fourth after Trulli pulled out a blinder and Raikkonen pipped him by 0.005s. Heikki slotted

↑ McLaren team boss Ron Dennis and Lewis embrace following the Brazilian Grand Prix and Hamilton's confirmation as Champion.

in fifth, but there was concern that Alonso would line up sixth, bristling with malevolent intent. If he could trip Lewis up, you knew he'd delight in doing so.

You felt that someone was overdoing the drama when, almost from nowhere, rain hit moments before the cars set off on their final formation lap. The start was postponed and, although the rain stopped as suddenly as it had started, everyone except Kubica changed to intermediates.

Lewis had to survive the first two corners and he did, helped by Heikki who was quicker away but tucked in behind him. Then Vettel pounced on Heikki and got by into Turn 4, with Alonso going around his outside. Lewis was safe in fourth, but Coulthard had been hit at Turn 2. So out came the safety car. Everything settled down, but not for long, as the track was drying and Fisichella was first in for dry tyres. Three laps later, with clear evidence that this was the right decision, Vettel and Alonso followed suit. Massa came in next time around and resumed in the lead, but Lewis stayed out a lap longer and fell to seventh as not only had Vettel and Alonso got by, but Fisichella too, up from 19th. Lewis demoted Trulli into Turn 1 on lap 13 then took an age to demote Fisichella and came under pressure from Glock.

Once past the Force India, Lewis was into that all-important fifth place. This became fourth when Vettel pitted from second. After the second round of stops, Vettel was back up to second and Lewis back down to fifth. That was enough to be champion, but were they all fuelled to end? No, and Vettel came in again on lap 51.

Then, with seven laps to go, rain fell... McLaren waited a few laps then brought Lewis in. Massa came in the next time around. Lewis was still fifth, but Vettel passed him on lap 69. Disaster! Sixth wouldn't be enough and Lewis was struggling for grip. There was no way that he could fight back, but there was one last hope. Glock hadn't come in for rain tyres. Lewis couldn't pass Vettel, but he might catch the Toyota driver. The team's global positioning system said that he ought to catch him on the final lap, but Massa and Ferrari were already celebrating. Then, with one corner to go, Vettel and Lewis flashed past Glock out of Juncao. You couldn't have cut it finer, Lewis had become the youngest ever world champion.

Lewis was the one at the wheel, but brother Nicolas and father Anthony were just as delighted that the name Hamilton could be added to the roll of F1 champions.

After those tumultuous closing laps, Lewis gathers his thoughts as he begins his celebrations as F1's 30th World Champion.

Returning to the pit lane, Lewis was stunned, unbelieving, hands trembling as he failed to reaffix his steering wheel as Heikki and Button congratulated him. Then he walked up the pit lane, too drained to say anything to the reporters before reaching the security of *parc ferme* and hugging everyone he could find to hug. The battle was won.

Lewis was measured rather than euphoric, numbed by how close he had been to being dealt a double dose of Brazilian heartbreak: "When it started to drizzle, I didn't want to take any risks - but Sebastian got past me and I was told that I had to get back in front of him. I couldn't believe it. Then at the very last corner I managed to get past Timo. It was amazing. I was shouting, 'Do I have it? Do I have it?' on the radio. It was only when I got to Turn 1 that the team told me I was world champion."

McLaren was ecstatic at the fruition of all the years of nurture it had invested in its favourite son, with Ron Dennis almost skipping as he spoke: "Well, that was a really tough race. We never did anything silly, but the rain made things extraordinarily tense. When Sebastian got past Lewis, we never gave up, and Lewis never gave up and took his chance brilliantly for one of the most thrilling finishes in sporting history."

There was universal respect for Massa's drive to victory and comment that Lewis had been lucky. This came not just from Ferrari fans, but even from racing great Sir Stirling Moss, who said: "Lewis was certainly lucky. He deserved the title, not for that race but for the season as a whole. He was too measured, and should have upped his pace a bit."

Former team owner Eddie Jordan reckoned he knew why Lewis came so close to falling at the final hurdle: "I don't think he went into the race in the right frame of mind. He was too defensive and didn't give himself a platform to take the championship from. He's at his best when he's attacking, as he's a great streetfighter. When he's defensive, Lewis isn't the best. In Brazil, he was two laps too late going to dry tyres and that put him in a precarious position." Yet, for all that, he'd done it: Lewis Hamilton, world champion, the youngest ever, the first black champion and certainly the most relieved.

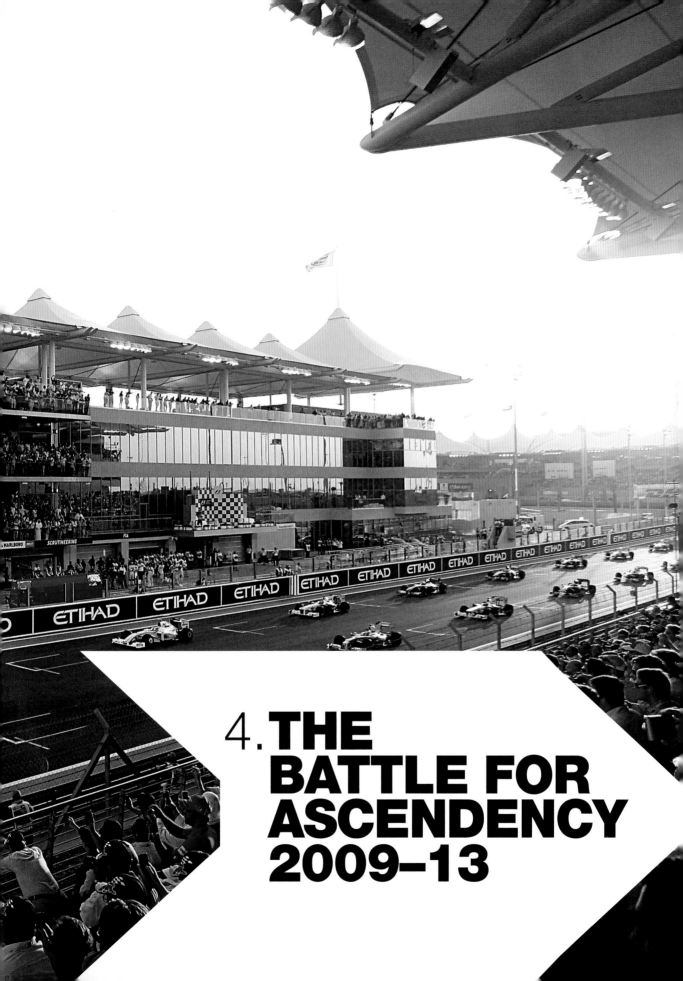

4. THE BATTLE FOR ASCENDENCY 2009–13

THE BATTLE FOR ASCENDENCY 2009–13

Having been pipped to the title in his rookie F1 season in 1997 and then clinching it at his second attempt, it would have taken a bold person to predict that no further titles would come Lewis's way over the next five campaigns. However, this is precisely what happened as Red Bull Racing took control. It was a chance for Lewis to see the other side of the coin.

With the long-desired F1 drivers' title in his possession, Lewis headed into 2009 with high hopes. There was a major rule change to contend with, but Lewis felt relaxed as he looked ahead to racing with the coveted No.1 on the nose of his McLaren. Little could he have known that a team that had closed its doors at the end of 2008, as the global economic crash started to bite, would not only be revived, but that it would also come up with a technical advantage that would leave every one of its rivals as also-rans.

That team was Brawn GP, born from the remains of the Honda team, and its use of a double-diffuser gave it a considerable performance advantage that enabled Jenson Button to dominate. Weirdly for Lewis, it left him with an uncompetitive car for the first time in his F1 career. "If your car's not competitive, you can't get out and push," he quipped. "All you can do is will your team on."

The MP4-24 was certainly not the best of the pack as F1 reverted to using slick tyres. There was also a major change to the technical regulations, introduced with the aim of making the racing more competitive by raising the diffuser, lowering the front wing, reducing the width of the rear wing (and raising its height), as well as stripping the cars of bargeboards and aerodynamic winglets to cut downforce. The rear wings were fitted with a driver-adjustable central flap that could be swivelled to cut their drag and give a driver a chance to get close enough to line up an overtaking manoeuvre, especially when used in conjunction with the kinetic energy release system that released energy stored after braking for bursts of an extra 80bhp.

The signs that the season was going to be a major challenge for McLaren were there in pre-season testing, as its MP4-24 was off the pace. And not only did Lewis start back in 18th at the opening round in Australia, but there was also trouble at the end of the race too, after he finished fourth – before Toyota's Jarno Trulli was disqualified from third. However, Trulli was then reinstated and Lewis was disqualified instead for not telling the stewards the truth about how Trulli passed him during a safety-car deployment to take third. This incident had ramifications, as long-standing McLaren team manager Davey Ryan was made

>> McLaren pitwork was a synchronized as ever in 2009, but there was little that Lewis could do about the pace of the innovative Brawn 001s.

"If your car's not competitive, you can't get out and push. All you can do is will your team on."

Lewis Hamilton

Lewis is joined on the podium in Turkey in 2010 by engineering director Paddy Lowe, team-mate Jenson Button and Red Bull Racing's Mark Webber.

Victory on the streets of Singapore after starting from pole position was a boost for Lewis's 2009 season, but he'd end the year fifth overall.

the fall guy for what happened, and Lewis later admitted that he was so upset he considered quitting over the incident.

The MP4-24 only became competitive midway through 2009 when development parts were introduced and Lewis had to wait until August before he won, at the Hungarian GP, with another victory coming in Singapore the round after he crashed on the last lap of the Italian GP when challenging Button for victory.

The battle within the team was rather less of a challenge, as Lewis dominated his team-mate Kovalainen for the second year running and very much enjoyed being McLaren's No.1 driver after the struggles he had with Alonso back in 2007.

The 2010 season marked the start of what would turn into the first of four successive drivers' titles for Sebastian Vettel with Red Bull Racing, but this championship was close. Even with the new points system – with 25 for a win rather than 10, and points awarded down to tenth rather than eighth – the top four drivers were covered by just 16 points after 19 rounds.

Button, Lewis's new team-mate, took two early-season wins before Lewis got going with a fortunate victory in Turkey – a race in which Red Bull Racing's Webber and Vettel clashed – and followed that up by winning next time out in Canada and adding a third victory in Belgium. This saw him finish fourth overall, 26 points and one position ahead of Button. However, had Lewis not crashed out of the races at Monza and Singapore, he would have placed higher, perhaps even been champion… Also, had the MP4-25 not fallen away increasingly from the pace, it would have been all the more likely that his title push would have reaped dividends.

The way the more easy-going Button had worked his way into the hearts of the crew was noticed by the F1 regulars. Most had felt that Button was going to be toasted by Lewis, but, instead, his self-confident decision to join Lewis's team paid off. It gave Lewis food for thought having had two years of facing no challenge from within his own camp when partnered by Kovalainen.

Rule changes for 2011 meant the reintroduction of KERS and Pirelli taking over from Bridgestone as F1's tyre supplier. What transpired out on the track was that Lewis had no answer to Vettel, particularly in the races.

It also was a year in which Lewis's team-mate Button finished three places

Contact with Kamui Kobayashi's Sauber on the approach to Spa-Francorchamps' Les Combes chicane led to this dramatic retirement from the 2011 Belgian GP.

"Lewis hadn't really sorted out a good work/life balance and there were times when he wasn't in a good place mentally."

Paddy Lowe

above him in the championship, despite both drivers taking three wins apiece. Many reckoned Button finished up higher placed as he appeared the more focused of the two. Not for the first time, Lewis's more high-profile life away from racing was seen by some as a distraction.

The tabloid media started to accuse Lewis of losing focus as he partied and enjoyed the jet-set lifestyle of a celebrity along with on-off girlfriend Nicole Scherzinger, a singer best known for leading the Pussycat Dolls. As a result, his protests when he failed to win were maybe afforded less sympathy than they might have been. Talk of a possible move to Red Bull Racing, in place of Mark Webber, was discussed, all of which unsettled Lewis even more.

Paddy Lowe, the long-time technical guru at McLaren, who would go on to join Mercedes before Lewis, reckoned he wasn't given an easy ride at the time: "He hadn't really sorted out a life/work balance, and there were some times when he was struggling, when he wasn't in a good place mentally."

There were some mistakes on the track, too, as well as the occasional less-intelligent moments, such as a flippant comment at Monaco when Lewis quipped about being penalized for causing an avoidable accident when he tipped Pastor Maldonado's Williams out of the race, asking "is it because I is black". It was a clumsy attempt at humour, lifting a quote made famous by comic character Ali G, but it served only to attract unnecessary attention. There was also an error of judgement in the Belgian GP when Lewis dived past Kamui Kobayashi's Sauber into Les Combes but hadn't left enough space and was pitched off into the barriers. Perhaps of more concern, though, was a series of clashes with Felipe Massa's Ferrari – at the Singapore, Japanese and Indian GPs. It had been a troublesome season, but Lewis

⌃ McLaren team principal Martin Whitmarsh congratulates Lewis on a rare success during the 2011 season.

» Victory at the 2011 Abu Dhabi GP was a boost after Sebastian Vettel had taken most of the season's trophies.

> ## "I leave McLaren with the greatest of memories, the best experiences and hopefully with a lot of good friends."
>
> **Lewis Hamilton**

ended it on a high with an exemplary victory in the penultimate round in Abu Dhabi.

With Mercedes power no match for Renault in 2012, Lewis and Button would end the year ranked fourth and fifth overall as Vettel completed his quickfire world championship treble. For much of the season, Lewis knew that he was moving on for 2013, yet he still delivered 100 per cent, especially in the second half of the campaign when updates to the MP4-27, introduced at the German GP, began to yield dividends. Lewis won in Canada and

⌃ Lewis walks the paddock with on-off girlfriend Nicole Scherzinger at a time when some questioned whether his jet-set lifestyle was affecting his form.

then, after the modifications, in Hungary, Italy and the United States – on F1's first visit to the all-new Circuit of the Americas, outside Austin.

There were moments of frustration, though, with Lewis causing friction when he was outqualified by Button at Spa-Francorchamps and then, in a fit of pique, tweeted his car's data readout to the public at large. Yet, there were moments when he really flew and, had it not been for mechanical failure while leading the Singapore and Abu Dhabi GPs, plus being taken out of the lead in the final race in Brazil, by Force India's Nico Hulkenberg, Lewis could have been world champion again. In many ways, this was his best championship since his title year in 2008.

At the end of the season, his departure from McLaren was definitely a defining moment in Lewis's career. "I really feel as if I'm leaving home and going elsewhere," he explained. "I've learnt my skills and I've now got all the right skills to go out and try something different. I leave McLaren with the greatest of memories, the best experiences and hopefully a lot of good friends."

Telling team boss Martin Whitmarsh of his decision to join Mercedes was, understandably, difficult. "When I called Martin, it was the most difficult call I've ever had to make, because we'd grown so close and he's been so supportive. I didn't want to let people down, but you have to let people down sometimes to make decisions."

So, it was all change for 2013, as Lewis joined childhood friend and kart-racing partner Nico Rosberg at Mercedes. This was always going to be "interesting", as Lewis used to be the quicker of the pair in karting and arrived at Mercedes with an F1 title under his belt. However, Rosberg was well established in the team,

Lewis had to make do with third place in the 2012 season-opener in Melbourne, a race won by McLaren team-mate Jenson Button.

Lewis leads into the first corner of the 2012 Brazilian GP, but he was to be spun out of the race by Nico Hulkenberg, shown behind Button's McLaren.

> ## "This year, I really struggled with the car, so I've not been able to reach my potential."
>
> ### Lewis Hamilton

having been there since it was created from Brawn GP for 2010, and had done well enough to put his illustrious team-mate Michael Schumacher in the shade.

Among those who thought Lewis's move to be a good one was none other than F1 legend Sir Stirling Moss, who said that he would have made the same move and reckoned that Lewis would soon be the team's lead driver.

Lewis's decision to leave McLaren, the team that had supported him from childhood and with which he had scored seven wins in 2012, to join Mercedes, who had enjoyed their first and only victory that season, inevitably sparked comment. Yet, it was clear that Lewis felt he would be able to be much more his own man with the German team, freeing himself from a perpetual pressure to conform that was spoiling both his enjoyment of his private life and the time he spent away from the track.

Life with Mercedes didn't necessarily provide a step forward. The car proved more competitive in qualifying than it did in races and Lewis struggled to master W04, especially its brakes. "I'd been at McLaren for a long time," said Lewis, "and every year I'd pretty much have the car built for me. The car was at the point where I could put it where I wanted it, as we'd tuned it for a long, long time. This year, I really struggled with the car, so I've not been able to reach my potential."

Despite his struggles, however, Lewis was delighted that the team made solid progress through the season – so much so he easily outscored both McLaren drivers (Button and Sergio Perez). Better still, Lewis ranked two places higher than Rosberg at season's end, although there wasn't much between them in fourth and sixth overall.

The move away from McLaren also marked a rebuilding of Lewis's relationship with his father, Anthony. It gave Lewis extra strength to take on the challenge of changing team. With the experience of spending a year settling into the way the team worked, greater personal contentment and a new set of regulations for 2014, Lewis knew there was every chance that his fortunes would change for the better.

⌃ Three-time World Champion Niki Lauda gave Lewis considerable encouragement after he joined Mercedes from McLaren in 2013.

» Lewis stands on his Mercedes W04 in Hungary in 2013 to celebrate his first victory for the team, a portent of things to come.

5. THE FORMULA ONE SEASON 2014

THE FORMULA ONE SEASON 2014

Mercedes had gained in form through 2013, but a major rule change for 2014 left the team with a new turbocharged engine that gave its drivers a spectacular advantage. With no rival team able

» Although no longer team-mates, Lewis remains good friends with Jenson Button as they head to the flatbed truck for a driver parade.

to live with Mercedes' chassis/engine combination, the title battle came down to a straight fight between team-mates, and Lewis came out ahead of Rosberg by taking 11 of the 16 wins they accumulated, with their rivals left trailing in their wake.

Any time there is a major change in the rulebook, there's a chance for a team to steal an advantage, and Lewis was supremely confident that Mercedes would be best prepared for the introduction of ERS (energy recovery systems) and hybrid engines. Indeed, there was clear expectation that Mercedes would be best set for 2014 and that Renault-powered Red Bull Racing wouldn't be able to give Sebastian Vettel the tools with which to gun for a fifth successive F1 title.

Lewis's confidence was well placed. Mercedes turned out to be very much on top of every one of these major changes but, while the performance was there for all to see and race wins were soon flowing, there were also some frustrating mechanical failures. For example, Lewis qualified on pole for the Australian GP, but dropped out of the lead of the opening race when the new V6 turbo stopped working after only two laps. Later, he came away with no points from the Canadian GP because of brake failure. His German GP was also hampered when his brakes failed in qualifying, leaving him to make his way forward from 20th to third. There was a similar outcome when he was forced to start from the back of the grid in Hungary after his engine caught fire before he could set a time in qualifying. These setbacks dented his championship challenge, but they weren't to prove damaging enough to derail his title hopes.

While Lewis and Rosberg learned how best to drive these new-style cars, with the different ways that they could use the squirts of an extra 160bhp at certain points around the lap from the stored heat and kinetic energy, they also made life tougher by getting at each other.

Their first clash came at the third round, the Bahrain GP. They arrived with a win apiece: Lewis's retirement from the opener in Melbourne handed victory to Rosberg, before the Briton recovered to win in Malaysia. Things were going well for Lewis at Sakhir. He was leading the final stint, but he was on medium tyres whereas Rosberg was on the softer, and thus faster, tyres. Given the help of a safety-car period, which enabled him to close onto Lewis's tail, the German was clearly

"The drivers are professional and you want to give them the opportunity to race, which is what we do."

Paddy Lowe

Angry at being denied pole, Lewis was still furious after Rosberg took victory two days later, with Red Bull's Daniel Ricciardo third.

It was all rather better natured four rounds earlier in the season when Lewis's victory in Malaysia put the Mercedes pair on one win apiece.

capable of lapping faster, but he was to remain frustrated as Lewis blocked him all the way to the finish, driving an inch-perfect race not to slip up under the intense pressure applied. It had been tough. As Lewis explained: "Keeping Nico out of my slipstream and the DRS was very hard. To be flat-out for ten laps, it was an exceptional race. Luckily, my tyres didn't go off in those last few laps."

There was talk that the team might end up with its drivers colliding as they both fought to win in this grand prix and subsequent ones, but Mercedes motorsport supremo Toto Wolff said that he wouldn't have it any other way. After all, he had been a racer himself in the past, and team orders were anathema to him. The team's technical director Paddy Lowe agreed. "Imposing team orders would be a terrible thing for F1," said the Cambridge engineering graduate. "It's something we owe to ourselves, owe to the sport, and we owe to the drivers. They're professionals and you want to give them the opportunity to race, which is what we do."

Another factor the drivers had to contend with in 2014 was having a reduced fuel capacity, this having been cut to 100kg (roughly 140 litres) per car per race. This meant that driving flat-out all race was no longer an option and the drivers had to work closely with their teams to ensure they matched their speed to their fuel load – that's to say didn't empty the tank before the end of the race by pressing on too much. Lewis acknowledged that it was a different way of going racing, and that he felt nostalgic for how F1 was when he graduated from GP2. "In 2007 and 2008, you could be pretty much flat the whole time, as they were flat-out stints. You might have to lift a tiny amount and coast to save fuel, but now it's a lot more strategic from a team's and driver's point-of-view."

With the 2014 rules, drivers had to decide at which point in the race they would go for it and at which point they would back off, short-shift the gears and come off the throttle as much as 50 metres earlier than before when approaching a

Lewis was a major draw at the Goodwood Festival of Speed, with fans enjoying being able to get up close in this less pressured environment.

"I was two and a half tenths of a second up on Nico on that qualifying lap [at Monaco] and didn't get to finish it."

Lewis Hamilton

braking zone. Going flat-out was no longer an option, as the rule-makers cut fuel consumption to give F1 a greener image. Lap times were obviously even further away from their zenith, 2004, when the cars were fitted with 3.5-litre V10 engines and were allowed to run with considerable downforce. Ask him privately, and it was plain that Lewis would rather be racing the ultimate spec F1 cars, but you can only race the equipment that is available to you, so he simply got on with it. Winning is always his motivation, so the target hadn't changed.

Monaco is a race in which Lewis has had a thin time by his own very high standards, having won on the streets of the principality just once in his first seven visits, doing so back in 2008. So, determined to improve his stats here, he went out to nail pole position, perhaps the most critical one of the whole year because of the paucity of overtaking opportunities the track offers in the race. Yet Lewis's final qualifying run, on which he was up on Rosberg by a couple of tenths of a second, was wrecked when Rosberg went off up the Mirabeau escape road just ahead of him, bringing out the yellow flags. Rosberg had been fastest on his first run in the final qualifying session, and Lewis was convinced his team-mate had gone off on purpose to scupper his pole bid. "I was two-and-a-half tenths up on that lap and didn't get to finish it," complained Lewis. The stewards investigated the incident and cleared Rosberg of any wrongdoing, but tensions between the pair rocketed, especially as Rosberg put pole to good use and raced to victory.

Lewis wasn't able to bounce back by winning the following race in Canada, as both Mercedes drivers were hit by engine management problems, with Lewis forced to retire with rear brake failure. Second place for Rosberg, behind Red Bull Racing's surprise first-time winner Daniel Ricciardo, left him with a 22-point championship lead over Lewis.

What followed on F1's return to Austria was even more gutting for Lewis as, on this occasion, Rosberg beat him fair and square. That Lewis had given himself an

⌃ The two Mercedes clashed on lap 2 at Spa-Francorchamps, with the team blaming Rosberg for the crash.

⌃ The backdrop was as scenic as ever as F1 returned to Austria, with Lewis advancing to second place from ninth.

« Lewis had every reason to be delighted at Monza after recovering from a poor start to catch and pass Rosberg for victory.

even bigger mountain to climb in Austria by spinning and so qualifying only ninth, was a major factor in the outcome. Impressively, the margin between the Mercedes drivers was only 2s at flagfall, but that was sufficient for Rosberg to extend his advantage to 29 points going into Lewis's home race.

Lewis has long admitted that winning the British GP is extra special to him, so he was relieved when he finally got to add another Silverstone victory to the one he achieved in dominant style in the wet/dry race in 2008. This time, Rosberg retired from the lead of the race with gearbox failure, but they were on very different race strategies and Lewis is confident he would have got past his team-mate anyway. When the chequered flag was flown, he was fully half a minute clear of Valtteri Bottas in the second-placed Williams, sending the crowd home happy. Considering Lewis had started from the third row, it was a great result. That he qualified so poorly was down to his decision to back off on his final lap, thinking he'd done enough for pole, only for the track to dry quickly and for Lewis to be bumped by five rivals.

The major flare-up between he and Rosberg came in the middle of the season, in the Hungarian GP, when Lewis refused an instruction from the team to let the German past. Lewis had made his final pitstop, but Rosberg had to pit once more and, having had to start the race from the rear of the grid after his car's engine caught fire before he could set a qualifying time, Lewis didn't want his team-mate to gain any advantage that might put him ahead. When the team supported Lewis's decision, it was Rosberg's turn to be livid. Mercifully, the pair had F1's three-week summer break to cool down.

Sadly, they didn't cool down enough. They clashed at the following race, at Spa-Francorchamps. Lewis was ahead as they approached Les Combes on lap 2 and Rosberg tried a passing move. It didn't work, but he seemed to leave the nose of his car there anyhow and took Lewis out. Rosberg's car was damaged, but he was at least able to continue. Mercedes was furious that Rosberg had handed victory to a rival team, fining him for turning a likely Mercedes one-two to just the 18 points he collected as he finished second behind Ricciardo.

"That was a very difficult scenario," said Lewis. "Years ago, I wouldn't have reacted the way I did. I'd have chosen another way that wouldn't have been a positive. Now, with age as well as maturing, I thought about it for the next few days and then turned my focus to a different area."

"Nico put up an incredible fight throughout the year ... We always said it would be amazing to be racing in the same team."

Lewis Hamilton

That focus was to bring Vettel's four-year reign to an end as Lewis secured his F1 second title. Mercedes was very much the engine to have in the first year of the new, 1.6-litre V6 turbo formula. He may have lost out in qualifying to Rosberg, taking seven poles to his team-mate's 11, but he delivered in the races, producing calm, accurate races of speed combined with strategy, with his move past Rosberg on the outside in the wet at Turn 1 midway through the Japanese GP standing out.

That was his third win in succession following his victories at Monza and in Singapore, and Lewis promptly added the next two, on F1's first visit to Sochi and then at the Circuit of the Americas. He then took second place behind

Not only did Lewis collect 25 points for victory in Singapore, but also Rosberg failed to score, putting Lewis three points in front.

This is the key moment from the first Russian GP as Rosberg dives past Lewis into Turn 2 on the opening lap but locks up.

Rosberg in the penultimate round in Brazil, after spinning just before his second pitstop, and then won the double-points finale in Abu Dhabi after Rosberg's pursuit was wrecked by the failure of his car's ERS, costing him 160bhp. He fell to 15th, and his failure to score gave Lewis a final points advantage of 67, 50 more than it had been when they'd arrived for the finale. No wonder Lewis had rubbed the sides of the cockpit late in the race, muttering "come on baby, we can make it". The tension had been relentless all year, but increasingly through the race weekend, from the chequered flag on, it was released. Afterwards, Rosberg was gracious in defeat, congratulating Lewis. It was a move he appreciated, saying: "Nico put up an incredible fight throughout the year. We met back in 1997 and we always said it would be amazing to be racing in the same team. After the race, he was very professional and said 'you drove really well.' And the same to him." Lewis knew that, had the failure that hit Nico's car hit his, then his team-mate would have been the one with the crown. It was that close.

Lewis then surprised many people by commenting that this title meant even more to him than his first one had done in 2008. It showed just how much the wilderness

"A lot of people said I'd made the wrong choice in coming to Mercedes, but the steps we took last year and this have been incredible. "

Lewis Hamilton

<< Hoisted high by his mechanics, Lewis celebrates in Abu Dhabi after landing this second F1 title with victory in the final race of the season.

^ Lewis's pet Roscoe has become one of the most famous bull dogs in the world after appearing with him at celebrity events.

years by his standards, from 2009 to 2013, had been weighing him down.

"A lot of people said I'd made the wrong choice in coming to Mercedes," said Lewis, "but the steps we took last year and then through this year have been incredible."

There had been occasions when Rosberg had used his pole positions well and won fair and square, but the balance in the races themselves was definitely with Lewis, so the right driver won the title.

In being crowned for a second time, Lewis felt special again. Not just as a grand prix winner, but as a champion again, and there's a massive difference in the satisfaction gained from that.

He also felt very proud of the way the team had moved to the top of the pile, commenting: "This is something incredibly special, what this team has put together, and I think that we've got great people in the right positions. I wanted to be a part of something that was building and growing and that would enjoy success in a way it hadn't really had before."

No team rests on its laurels, however, and Lowe summed up 2014 by saying: "If we analyze the whole season, we weren't as reliable as we should have been and, as you can't take anything for granted over the winter in F1, we'll have to do our best and see where we turn up next year."

6. THE FORMULA ONE SEASON 2015

THE FORMULA ONE SEASON 2015

Having two F1 drivers' titles put Lewis in exalted company, but he wanted more: wanted to join the greats. In the end, Lewis claimed his third title with three rounds to spare, but his route to getting there was far rockier than he would have liked, with almost all of the friction coming from within the Mercedes camp as his tussle with Rosberg became increasingly tetchy and troubled.

Relaxed by having finally put the "wilderness years" of 2009 to 2013 behind him when he failed to add to his 2008 drivers' title, Lewis had strong ambitions for 2015 and was determined to do even more to achieve them. Close-season testing had proved that Mercedes had a performance advantage once again and the drivers were encouraged that one of the key aims for the Mercedes W06 was improved reliability With Lewis's target clearly set on landing a third title, his first target was to make every single lap count when out on the track. "I'll be working to improve in FP1, FP2 and FP3, as they are all areas that need to be strengthened," said Lewis. "Last year, if I'd done better in qualifying, it would have made the races easier."

Improve in qualifying he did, with Lewis taking pole position at 11 of the first 12 rounds, missing out only at the Circuit de Catalunya. From these 11 poles, he went on to win seven grands prix, in Australia, China, Bahrain, Canada, Britain, Belgium and Italy, setting himself fair for a shot at a third drivers' title. Monaco could have been a win too, but the team made a tactical blunder by bringing him in for a pitstop during a safety-car deployment and that dropped Lewis from first to third as he emerged behind Rosberg and Vettel, with no chance to reverse the situation in the remaining 14 laps. Lewis was bamboozled, saying: "I can't express the way I feel at the moment. I saw the team out in the pitlane on the screens and thought Nico was pitting. So I came in with full confidence that the others had done the same. This is a race that is close to my heart, so I really wanted to win." Clearly, a second Monaco win to add to his one there in 2008 will have to wait.

⌃ Lewis is congratulated by podium MC Arnold Schwarzenegger after winning the season-opening race in Melbourne's Albert Park.

≫ New season, new hairstyle as Lewis sports a beard for 2015, with his distinctive styles very much part of his personal appeal.

Diving down the incline into Turn 3 at Shanghai, with Rosberg behind him, Lewis heads off towards a win in China that proved Mercedes was in control.

Lewis is congratulated by Kimi Raikkonen after they finished first and second in the fourth round, Bahrain's first night race.

What was clear from the outset, though, was that the Mercedes V6 turbo was still the pick of the pack, and that its class-leading power output allowed the four teams using it scope to run with more wing angle than their rivals. This certainly was a huge help. For all that, however, Lewis had no ambitions for a runaway win in the title battle. At the start of the season, he was sure that rival teams would cut into Mercedes' advantage in 2015, but he still wanted to fight for glory. "I always want to be able to enjoy the battle," he explained. "That's ultimately what I live for." In truth, the tighter the battle, the more Lewis delivers.

Pure speed has always been a key component in his skill set and, when analyzing that speed, Lewis remains convinced there is no secret to it, saying: "I can only put my speed down to the natural way that I drive. I put it down to talent." Despite that, he also acknowledges that hard 'work is involved too: "You're constantly developing your driving. You have to."

After sports psychologist Don Macpherson had said in 2014 that Lewis was too focused on winning rather than on the process of winning, Lewis set himself the target of finding ever better ways to work with his engineers in 2015. Chief among his wishes in this regard was translating his feelings about the car's handling into making the right changes to improve the car. The proof of Lewis's success in this is shown by how the wins kept flowing, as his blossoming working relationship with the team, combined with ever more experience and maturity now that his twenties were behind him, became more and more evident. Furthermore, after coping with the break-up of his relationship with Nicole Scherzinger, something that can never be easy for anyone occupying the public spotlight, Lewis was clearly more settled in his personal life.

Every racing campaign will produce moments of frustration, such as when his hopes of winning at Monaco were scuppered by a tactical blunder, but Lewis also kept on course by relying on his strong religious faith that things happen for a reason. He said that the outcome of this was not exploding with rage when failing to win. Not coming first is always a problem for top sportspeople, but, undoubtedly, experience is key to learning how to cope with the disappointment.

"After a race, you're excited, but you don't want to show too much excitement,"

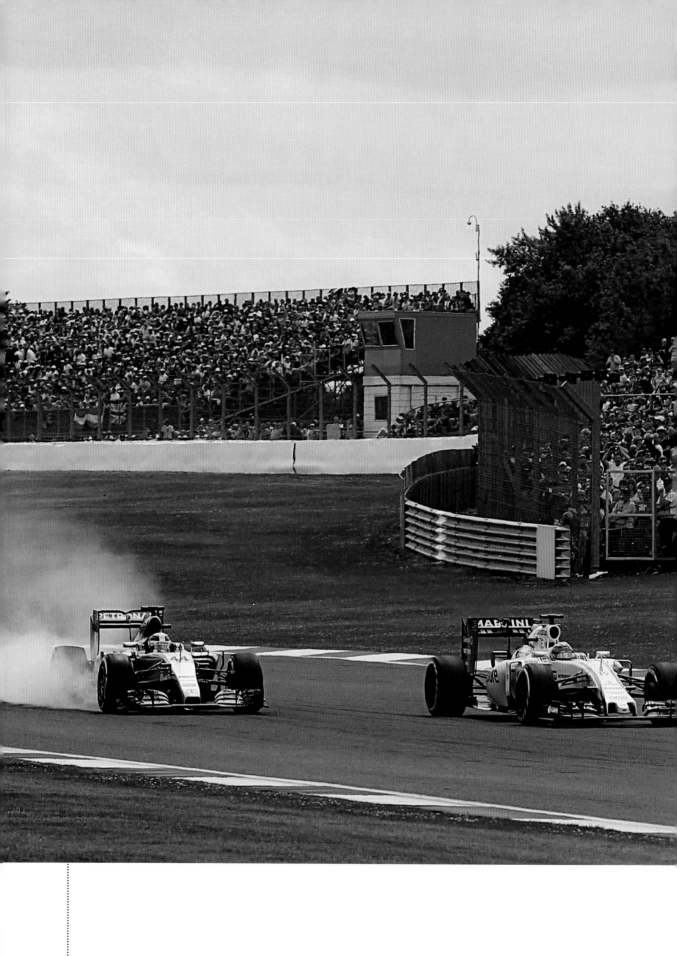

Lewis told respected journalist David Tremayne, "or you might be disappointed and don't want to show too much disappointment, as you know your team-mate, or whoever else is there, will get energy from that."

Back in his rookie F1 season in 2007, Lewis found such a task far from easy to manage and says that it used to take him up to a week to recover from any loss. The most keenly felt disappointment comes, of course, from a mistake made rather than a mechanical failure. After all, there's no point in beating yourself up for something that's not your fault.

There were plenty of good times for him to enjoy in 2015. By adding further victories in Japan, Russia and then the USA, to take his tally to ten wins, the title was his with three rounds still to run. In those final three races, though, pole and victory went each time to Rosberg, prompting comment from some quarters that Lewis was partying too much, notably after he was late arriving in Brazil after a road collision in Monaco in the early hours of a morning. However, that may not have been the reason for this dip in form at all, as Lewis would later point out that he had struggled to get to grips with set-up changes made following the Singapore GP, at which the team failed to get its cars to work on Pirelli's softest tyres.

Whether being beaten by Rosberg in those last three races gives Lewis a less relaxing winter break remains to be seen. Only he will know.

On what he does away from the track, seemingly living a celebrity high life, is largely irrelevant, and F1 would be very much the poorer without the image with which he adorns it. Those who decry Lewis for hanging out with stars of music and fashion should consider the fact that he doesn't remain cocooned within F1 and has actually added to his maturity and ability to react to situations by stepping into and interacting with an adult world beyond the track.

Lewis told Tremayne that he had struck a really good balance between working hard and playing hard, and was really enjoying it, saying: "At some points you are really on the limit and turn up a bit tired. But then I get energy from my fans, from the team, get in the car and feel great." So, he has no plans to change.

Any impression Lewis may give of it all being rather easy is just an image, as he readily admits that for an F1 driver to be on top of their game is no easy matter. He told *Autosport F1* reporter Lawrence Barretto that "being in the zone" for an entire grand prix weekend was really draining. "Getting in the zone is making sure you get sleep, eat well, understand how your body feels and if you feel clear in your mind. It's about putting your phone down. It's about thinking clearly, making

↟ Lewis's win at the British GP was the answer to his prayers as it extended his advantage over team-mate Rosberg to 17 points.

≫ The Mercedes crew applaud Lewis as he drives the wrong way down the pitlane to parc ferme after winning the Belgian GP.

sure you have done your due diligence, understood your notes. If your mind is clouded by other stuff, then you're not in the zone."

Triple world champion Jackie Stewart would agree with that, saying that to achieve repeated success, a driver needs "mind over matter, mind over enthusiasm".

One element of his arsenal that impresses the sport's insiders is his ability to feel the grip available, with F1 racer turned TV analyst Martin Brundle highlighting how Lewis is able to adapt to the changes as his fuel load lightens, and the tyres come and go and the track changes. Brundle also has great admiration for Lewis's ability to be a bit of a streetfighter when the moment to strike arrives.

Fellow TV pundit Anthony Davidson reckons this ability to adapt is a key to his race advantage over Rosberg: "When you're going through the race, with changeable conditions," said the ex-Minardi and Super Aguri racer, "there's no way that you can stop and have a look at the data. You're out there, having to survive by yourself."

Lewis travelled to the 16th round, the United States GP, knowing that he could secure his third title at the Circuit of the Americas, and he duly completed the job by scooping the 25 points for victory, but it wasn't straightforward. For starters, a hurricane hit, and so qualifying was delayed until race morning. Rosberg bagged pole, but he was slow away and this allowed Lewis to make a dive up the inside into Turn 1. Not only did he get through, but he pushed Rosberg wide and both Red Bulls demoted the German as well. However, the race was punctuated by safety-car periods caused by incidents on a wet/dry track and Rosberg gained an advantage by pitting during one of these deployments and so found himself in the lead, only to slip up under pressure from Lewis and slide off at Turn 12. He was able to rejoin, but the race and the title were Lewis's.

"Getting in the zone is making sure you get sleep, eat well, understand how your body feels and if you feel clear in your mind."

Lewis Hamilton

"Lewis was trying to drive me off the track, but I wasn't moving because I have the right to the track there."

Nico Rosberg

Asked about their first-corner clash, Lewis explained: "It wasn't intentional. We both braked very deep and I understood he was on the outside and, in the wet, that's where the grip is. He was turning and I wasn't, so we touched." Rosberg wasn't impressed: "He was trying to drive me off the track, but I wasn't moving because I have the right to the track there."

Looking to provide an overview, Wolff concluded: "It was wet and so the car was hard to control, but it was too hard on Lewis's side."

However, what really counted to Lewis was that he was World Champion for a third time, thus matching the achievement of his childhood hero Ayrton Senna. "I remember my first British (kart) championship, where my dad and I drove home singing 'We Are The Champions', and now it's just crazy to think that I'm a three-time World Champion."

Having had to fight so hard to find the money to get established in the sport, Lewis understands implicitly that his success isn't all about just him, and he was eager to outline this point. "I owe it all to my dad, to my family who sacrificed so much for me to be here," he grinned. "I realize that while I get to enjoy driving an F1 car, this is really a platform for me to inspire young people never to give up on their dreams. Today, there were so many times I thought I'd lost the race, but never for one second gave up."

The last three races, in Mexico, Brazil and Abu Dhabi, didn't go to plan, well Lewis's plan, as Rosberg took pole and won all three, with Lewis second each time, making his displeasure known over the radio when the team wouldn't let him change his strategy in an attempt to usurp Rosberg. It added to the excitement for TV viewers, as they waited to discover whether the team would comply. They were to be disappointed on each occasion.

« Lewis holds the lead ahead of Sebastian Vettel's Ferrari as Rosberg gets pushed back down to sixth place at the start of the Italian GP.

⌄ Lewis looks less than happy as Rosberg explains how he claimed pole position for the Japanese GP at Suzuka.

It's celebration time in the Mercedes garage after victory at the Circuit of the Americas – his 10th of the season – enabled Lewis to claim his third F1 title.

"I've had the honour of watching some of the greatest drivers of all time, and Lewis justifies winning three world championships."

Sir Jackie Stewart

As a parting shot, Lewis was asked after final round at the Yas Marina Circuit whether he or Nico would go into the close season with a better frame of mind. His replay was a classic: "I think being World Champion sounds a lot better than race winner." Rosberg knows that too, and also knows that the 2016 season might be his last chance of title glory, as rival teams might close the performance gap.

There was also another cloud on the horizon as, after the last race of the season, fed up by the bickering between his drivers, Mercedes motorsport supremo Toto Wolff warned that either driver, or both, could be shown the door, as their sniping was the team's biggest weakness.

That storm may blow over, but Britain's only other triple F1 World Champion, Jackie Stewart, is best-placed to summarize Lewis's remarkable achievement in matching his tally of titles. "I've had the opportunity of watching some of the greatest drivers of all time, from Fangio to Ascari to Moss to Clark, Lauda and obviously Senna," says the Scot, "and Lewis justifies winning three world championships. There have been times when there have been a larger number of top-line drivers all shooting for the title, but it didn't happen for Schumacher or for Vettel. However, you still have to drive the car and Lewis drives extremely well."

Lewis has moved past Vettel in the listings for the number of wins, his 43 putting him behind only Schumacher (91) and Alain Prost (51), with the latter knowing that he could be toppled in 2016 and that Lewis could join both he and Vettel as one of F1's three four-time world champions. Lewis has also demoted Vettel to fourth in the pole rankings by advancing his tally to 49 to put him 16 behind Senna. In terms of points scored, only Vettel remains ahead of Lewis, by just 29.

Will a fourth title come Lewis's way in 2016? Only time will tell, and Vettel could challenge for Ferrari, but you wouldn't want to bet against it. With a Mercedes contract for 2017 and 2018 as well, more records are sure to tumble.

Rosberg holds the inside line at the start of the race in Brazil and he was to stay in front all race.

Mexicans love wrestling and Lewis took part in an unusual PR event ahead of the race in Mexico City.

RECORDS & STATISTICS

Lewis Hamilton's record as he rose through the ranks from cadet kart racer to grand prix winner has been astonishing. His career stats show how he claimed 16 titles and collected more than 300 trophies, but it hasn't been victory every time out, as there have been periods of learning and adjustment as he graduated to more advanced categories before he put it all together, bested his rivals and was crowned champion again.

1993 CADET KARTS
1994 CADET KARTS
1995 CADET KARTS
  British champion; STP Cadet champion
1996 CADET KARTS
  McLaren Mercedes Champions of the Future champion; Sky TV
  Kart Masters champion; Five Nations champion
1997 JUNIOR YAMAHA KARTS
  McLaren Mercedes Champions of the Future champion; British champion
1998 JICA (Junior Intercontinental A) KARTS
  McLaren Mercedes Champions of the Future runner-up;
  Italian Open series, fourth
1999 JICA & ICA (Intercontinental A) KARTS
  Italian Industrials ICA champion; European JICA runner-up; Italian JICA
  Open series, fourth; Trophy de Pomposa JICA winner;
2000 FORMULA A KARTS
  World No 1; World Cup champion; European champion; Winner of Elf Masters
2001 FORMULA SUPER A KARTS
  World Championship, 15th
  BRITISH FORMULA RENAULT WINTER SERIES with Manor Motorsport

Starts	Poles	Wins	Fastest laps	Rank
4	0	0	0	5th

2002 BRITISH FORMULA RENAUL with Manor Motorsport

Starts	Poles	Wins	Fastest laps	Rank
13	3	3	4	3rd

  FORMULA RENAULT EUROCUP with Manor Motorsport

Starts	Poles	Wins	Fastest laps	Rank
4	1	1	1	5th

2003 BRITISH FORMULA RENAULT with Manor Motorsport

Starts	Poles	Wins	Fastest laps	Rank
17	11	10	9	1st

  BRITISH FORMULA 3 with Manor Motorsport

Starts	Poles	Wins	Fastest laps	Rank
2	0	0	0	n/r

2004   FORMULA 3 EUROSERIES with Manor Motorsport

Starts	Poles	Wins	Fastest laps	Rank
20	1	1	2	5th

2005   FORMULA 3 EUROSERIES with ASM

Starts	Poles	Wins	Fastest laps	Rank
20	13	15	10	1st

2006   GP2 with ART Grand Prix

Starts	Poles	Wins	Fastest laps	Rank
21	1	5	7	1st

2007   FORMULA 1 with McLaren Mercedes

Starts	Poles	Wins	Fastest laps	Rank
17	6	4	2	2nd

2008   FORMULA 1 with McLaren Mercedes

Starts	Poles	Wins	Fastest laps	Rank
18	7	5	1	1st

2009   FORMULA 1 with McLaren Mercedes

Starts	Poles	Wins	Fastest laps	Rank
17	4	2	0	5th

2010   FORMULA 1 with McLaren Mercedes

Starts	Poles	Wins	Fastest laps	Rank
19	1	3	5	4th

2011   FORMULA 1 with McLaren Mercedes

Starts	Poles	Wins	Fastest laps	Rank
19	1	3	3	5th

2012   FORMULA 1 with McLaren Mercedes

Starts	Poles	Wins	Fastest laps	Rank
20	7	4	1	4th

2013   FORMULA 1 with Mercedes AMG

Starts	Poles	Wins	Fastest laps	Rank
19	5	1	1	4th

2014   FORMULA 1 with Mercedes AMG

Starts	Poles	Wins	Fastest laps	Rank
19	7	11	7	1st

2015   FORMULA 1 with Mercedes AMG

Starts	Poles	Wins	Fastest laps	Rank
19	11	10	8	1st

CAREER TOTALS IN FORMULA 1

Starts	Poles	Wins	Fastest laps	Titles
167	49	43	28	3

CREDITS

The publishers would like to thank the following sources for their kind permission to reproduce the pictures in this book.

Getty Images: /Ronaldo Schemidt/AFP: 124; Karwai Tang/WireImage: 109

LAT Photographic: 57; /Lorenzo Bellanca: 50; /Bloxham: 20; /Sam Bloxham: 104; /Charles Coates: 49, 54, 86, 97, 103, 113; /Chris Dixon: 23, 28; /Glenn Dunbar: 11, 12, 32, 38, 59, 64, 78-79, 107, 112, 119, 125; /Jakob Ebrey: 94-95; /Steve Etherington: 2, 7, 43, 45, 52, 63, 81, 83, 84-85, 87, 89, 92, 93, 99, 102, 108, 110-111, 114, 115, 118, 120, 122-123, 128; /Andrew Ferraro: 4-5, 39, 66, 72, 77, 82, 90-91; /Gary Hawkins: 100-101; /Andrew Hone: 106; /Andre Irlmeier: 35, 37; /Alastair Staley: 98; /Steven Tee: 40-41, 46, 60-61, 69, 73, 75, 76, 88, 116, 121

PA Images: /Sutton Motorsport: 14-15, 19, 24, 29, 30, 34

REX Shutterstock: 25, 27; /Anglia Press Agency: 8, 17, 21; /Philip Brown: 22

Every effort has been made to acknowledge correctly and contact the source and/or copyright holder of each picture and Carlton Books Limited apologises for any unintentional errors or omissions which will be corrected in future editions of this book.

❯❯ Lewis looks over the pitwall to check out the weather conditions as well as to wave to the fans.